D0174810

The Greatest Gift

The Greatest Gift
UNWRAPPING THE FULL
LOVE STORY OF CHRISTMAS

ANN VOSKAMP

Tyndale House Publishers, Inc.
Carol Stream, Illinois

Visit Tyndale online at www.tyndale.com.

TYNDALE and Tyndale's quill logo are registered trademarks of Tyndale House Publishers, Inc.

The Greatest Gift: Unwrapping the Full Love Story of Christmas

Copyright © 2013 by Ann Voskamp. All rights reserved.

Cover photograph taken by Stephen Vosloo. Copyright © by Tyndale House Publishers, Inc. All rights reserved. Cut paper illustrations copyright © 2013 by Paula Doherty. All rights reserved. Author photograph taken by Molly Morton-Sydorak, copyright © 2012. All rights reserved.

Designed by Julie Chen

Published in association with William K. Jensen Literary Agency, 119 Bampton Court, Eugene, Oregon 97404.

Unless otherwise indicated, Scripture quotations are taken from the *Holy Bible*, New Living Translation, copyright © 1996, 2004, 2007, 2013 by Tyndale House Foundation. Used by permission of Tyndale House Publishers, Inc., Carol Stream, Illinois 60188. All rights reserved.

Scripture quotations marked NIV are taken from the Holy Bible, *New International Version,*® *NIV.*® Copyright © 1973, 1978, 1984, 2011 by Biblica, Inc.™ Used by permission of Zondervan. All rights reserved worldwide. www.zondervan.com. (Some quotations may be from the previous edition of the NIV, copyright © 1984.)

Scripture quotations marked ESV are taken from *The Holy Bible*, English Standard Version® (ESV®), copyright © 2001 by Crossway, a publishing ministry of Good News Publishers. Used by permission. All rights reserved.

Scripture quotations marked NJB are taken from *The New Jerusalem Bible*. Copyright © 1985 by Darton, Longman & Todd, Ltd. and Doubleday & Co., Inc.

Scripture quotations marked KJV are taken from the *Holy Bible*, King James Version.

Scripture quotations marked NKJV are taken from the New King James Version.® Copyright © 1982 by Thomas Nelson, Inc. Used by permission. All rights reserved.

Scripture quotations marked NASB are taken from the New American Standard Bible,® copyright © 1960, 1962, 1963, 1968, 1971, 1972, 1973, 1975, 1977, 1995 by The Lockman Foundation. Used by permission.

Scripture quotations marked WEY are taken from the Weymouth New Testament. Public domain.

Library of Congress Cataloging-in-Publication Data

Voskamp, Ann, date.
  The greatest gift : unwrapping the full love story of Christmas / Ann Voskamp.
    pages cm
  ISBN 978-1-4143-8708-6 (hc)
  1. Advent—Prayers and devotions. I. Title.
  BV40.V67 2014
  242'.33—dc23   2013017996

Printed in the United States of America

19   18   17   16   15   14   13
 8   7   6   5   4   3

Contents

Your Invitation to Unwrap the Gift

❄

Big and glossy and loud and fast—that's how this bent-up world turns.

But God, when He comes—He shows up in this fetal ball.

He who carved the edges of the cosmos curved Himself into a fetal ball in the dark, tethered Himself to the uterine wall of a virgin, and lets His cells divide, light splitting all white.

He gave up the heavens that were not even large enough to contain Him and lets Himself be held in a hand.

The mystery so large becomes the Baby so small, and infinite God becomes infant.

The Giver becomes the Gift, this quiet offering.

This heart beating in the chest cavity of a held child,

a thrumming heart beating hope, beating change, beating love, beating the singular song you've been waiting for—that the whole dizzy planet's been spinning round waiting for.

Waiting.

Advent.

It comes from the Latin.

It means "coming."

When you open the pages of Scripture to read of His coming, of this first Advent, before you ever read of the birth of Jesus, you always have the genealogy of Jesus.

It's the way the Gift unwraps: you have Christ's family tree . . . before you have a Christmas tree. If you don't come to Christmas through Christ's family tree and you come into the Christmas story just at the Christmas tree—this is hard, to understand the meaning of His coming.

Because without the genealogy of Christ, the limbs of His past, the branches of His family, the love story of His heart that has been coming for you since before the beginning—how does Christmas and its tree stand? Its roots would be sheared. Its meaning would be stunted. The arresting pause of the miracle would be lost.

Because in the time of prophets and kings, the time of Mary and Joseph, it wasn't your line of credit, line of work, or line of accomplishments that explained who you were.

It was your family line. It was family that mattered. Family gives you context, and origin gives you understanding, and the family tree of Christ always gives you hope.

The coming of Christ was right through families of messed-up monarchs and battling brothers, through affairs and adultery and more than a feud or two, through skeletons in closets and cheaters at tables. It was in that time of prophets and kings, the time of Mary and Joseph, that men were in genealogies and women were invisible. But for Jesus, women had names and stories and lives that mattered.

The family tree of Christ startlingly notes not one woman but four. Four broken women—women who felt like outsiders, like has-beens, like never-beens. Women who were weary of being taken advantage of, of being unnoticed and uncherished and unappreciated; women who didn't fit in, who didn't know how to keep going, what to believe, where to go—women who had thought about giving up. And Jesus claims exactly these who are wandering and wondering and wounded and worn out as *His*. He grafts you into His line and His story and His heart, and He gives you His name, His lineage, His righteousness. He graces you with plain grace.

Is there a greater Gift you could want or need or have?

Christ comes right to your Christmas tree and looks at

your family tree and says, "I am your God, and I am one of you, and I'll be the Gift, and I'll take you. *Take Me?*"

This, *this*, is the love story that's been coming for you since the beginning.

It is possible for you to miss it.

To brush past it, to rush through it, to not see how it comes for you up over the edges of everything, quiet and unassuming and miraculous—how every page of the Word has been writing it, reaching for you, coming for you. And you could wake on Christmas only to grasp that you never took the whole of the Gift, the wide expanse of grace. So now we pause. Still. Ponder. Hush. Wait. Each day of Advent, He gives you the gift of time, so you have time to be still and wait.

Wait for the coming of the God in the manger who makes Himself bread for us near starved.

For the Savior in swaddlings who makes Himself the robe of righteousness for us worn out.

For Jesus, who makes precisely what none of us can but all of us want: Christmas.

Sometimes the heart waiting for the Gift . . . is the art of the Gift.

This waiting, your art—mark it.

Mark Advent with a counting, a way of staying awake and not missing.

It could happen like the numbering of time, like the rings on a tree.

Like a leaning over that Jesse Tree of the Old Testament, that Jesse Tree axed down, and counting rings down to the greatest Gift, to life out of the dream cut off.

That Jesse Tree, named after Jesse, who was the father of David—David to whom God promised that his line and his sons and his family would reign forever without end.

And when David's sons and grandsons and great-grandsons turned from God and loved the gifts and the flesh more than the Giver and the Father—their kingdoms fell. Their homes fell apart.

It looked as if the whole family tree of Jesse had been chopped right off at the roots. But God . . .

But our covenant-keeping, promise-keeping God vowed, "Out of the stump of David's family will grow a shoot—yes, a new Branch bearing fruit from the old root. . . . In that day the heir to David's throne will be a banner of salvation to all the world. The nations will rally to him, and the land where he lives will be a glorious place" (Isaiah 11:1, 10).

Out of the stump of our hearts . . .

In this day, this season, miracles will grow within, unfurl, bear fruit.

And the heart that makes time and space for Him to come will be a glorious place.

A place of sheer, radiant defiance in the face of a world careening mad and stressed.

Because each day of Advent, we will actively wait.

We will wait knowing that the remaking of everything has already begun.

We will linger over the lines of the Old Testament stories, tracing the branches of the family tree of Christ, the spreading pageantry of humankind, from Adam to the Messiah—each historical truth pointing to the coming, the already relief, the incarnation of God.

We'll still and slow and trace each exquisite ornament pictured with these twenty-five Advent narratives, each ornament cut slow out of paper.

And there He is—the exquisite Gift cut and given for us, broken.

The Gift who hung on a Tree for us, cut off.

The Gift who was pierced for you, wounded—your wounded, willing God, who unfolds Himself on the Tree as your endless, greatest Gift.

Ann Voskamp

Jesse Tree Invitation and Instructions

❄

So. It's late November, and you'll need your Jesse Tree to wait for Jesus' coming. To come to the Christmas tree through the family tree of Christ.

Your Jesse Tree may take on a number of wondrous forms. A silhouette of a tree may be sewn or painted, cut out of felt, or quilted. It may be hung from the fridge, a wall, a door, a window.

Or you may use a small evergreen tree in an urn, a cluster of red dogwood branches in a vase, or a pot of hemlock, pine, spruce, sticks, or holly.

The ornaments can be downloaded from my website (using the code JESSE) and then printed out to hang on any tree of your imagining or envisioning. Just whatever you do . . .

Anticipate Christ . . . and Celebrate Christmas, His Coming

All this Jesse Tree making? It's a bit like making your own family tree—a family tree with its arching branches of grandfathers and grandmothers, its sheltering leaves of aunts and uncles. To make a Jesse Tree is to trace the family line and heritage of your own forever family—the family of God.

Out of the stump of David's family will grow a shoot.

ISAIAH 11:1

December 1

It Is Advent: Come

Today's Reading

Out of the stump of David's family will grow a shoot—
>   yes, a new Branch bearing fruit from the old root.
And the Spirit of the LORD will rest on him—
>   the Spirit of wisdom and understanding,
the Spirit of counsel and might,
>   the Spirit of knowledge and the fear of the
>   LORD. . . .

In that day the heir to David's throne
>   will be a banner of salvation to all the world.
The nations will rally to him,
>   and the land where he lives will be a glorious
>   place.

ISAIAH 11:1-2, 10

The mattering part is never what isn't.

The mattering part is never the chopped-off stump.

It isn't what dream has been cut down, what hope has been cut off, what part of the heart has been cut out.

The tender mattering part is—*you have a Tree.*

Out of the last and forgotten son of Jesse comes forth one tender branch that will grow into a crown of thorns . . . a rugged cross . . . your ladder back to God. Jesus will go to *impossible* lengths to rescue you.

Out of the stump of that fallen tree, watered with the living waters that flow from the depths of His grace, a twig sprouts. That twig will be the scepter that defeats your sin . . . and lets you grow again.

Out of that stump and the sheared impossible there springs a singular shoot—tender and vulnerable.

There, here, in the midst of the inconceivable, the loud claims, the hard sells, the big spectacles, Christ comes small, the micro- macro-miracle who comes in the whisper and says, *Seek Me.* Just where you are, look for the small glimpses of God-glory breaking in, breaking out, sprouting, shooting, unfurling, bearing fruit, making a Kingdom, remaking the world. Slow and still. And seek the shoot that bears witness to God—the hardly noticed child, the hymn hummed over the sink, the unassuming woman bent at the register, the dog-eared Word of God beckoning from the shelf.

Gaze on shoots of glory to grow deep roots in God.

The theology of the Tree, of the Cross, always seeks the presence of God in the belittled gifts of the world.

The small Babe of Bethlehem, the dismissed Son of God, the stripped and beaten Messiah hanging exposed on the Tree—He begs us to spend the attention of Advent on the little, the least, the lonely, the lost.

Because in the rush, in the hurry, in our addiction to speed—it might just be a bit like stepping on the shoot that sprouts from the stump.

Advent, it is made of the moments.

This slow unfurling of grace.

Unwrapping More of His Love in the World

Plant wheat or grass seeds for every act of love and kindness you do today. Continue planting seeds for kindnesses throughout the Jesse Tree journey. Keep watering the sprouts until Christmas Eve. You're growing straw for the manger of the coming King! Love and new life are coming!

In the silence of a midwinter dusk, there is far off in the deeps of it somewhere a sound so faint that for all you can tell it may be only the sound of the silence itself. You hold your breath to listen. You walk up the steps to the front door. The empty windows at either side of it tell you nothing, or almost nothing. For a second you catch a whiff in the air of some fragrance that reminds you of a place you've never been and a time you have no words for. You are aware of the beating of your heart. The extraordinary thing that is about to happen is matched only by the extraordinary moment just before it happens. Advent is the name of that moment.

FREDERICK BUECHNER

A Moment for Reflection

In what ways do you feel like a lifeless stump, longing for
a tender shoot of hope?

....

....

....

....

What are you waiting for, yearning for this season?

....

....

....

....

Where can you see new life coming in what you may have
considered dead?

....

....

....

....

....

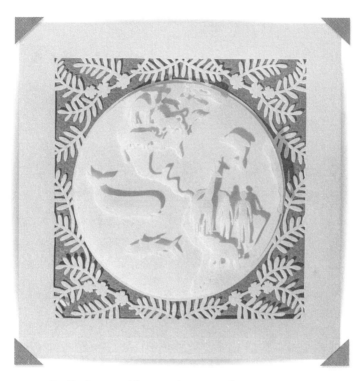

So God created human beings in his own image.

GENESIS 1:27

December 2

Life Begins as a Love Story

Today's Reading

In the beginning God created the heavens and the earth. The earth was formless and empty, and darkness covered the deep waters. And the Spirit of God was hovering over the surface of the waters.

Then God said, "Let there be light," and there was light. And God saw that the light was good. Then he separated the light from the darkness. God called the light "day" and the darkness "night." . . .

God said, "Let us make human beings in our image, to be like us. They will reign over the fish in the sea, the birds in the sky, the livestock, all the wild animals on the earth, and the small animals that scurry along the ground."

So God created human beings in his own image.
   In the image of God he created them;
   male and female he created them.

GENESIS 1:1-5, 26-27

This Christmas story—it begins in the beginning, this love story that's been coming for you since the beginning.

It begins with the always coming of Christ.

Christ, who is there in the beginning, the voice calling out of darkness, an echo in cosmic emptiness, speaks it by the commanding word of His mouth: *Let there be . . .*

Let there be light and land and living beasts. . . .

But you? You alone were formed by a huddle of hearts: *Let us make human beings.*

The authority of God made all of creation. But it was the *affection* of God that made all His children.

The three persons of the Trinity—Father God, Jesus Christ, and Holy Spirit—gathered close together to imagine you. And God in three persons, uncontainable affection, knelt down and kissed warm life into you with the breath of His love.

You are made of the dust of this earth, and you are made of the happiness of heaven, and you are flesh and you are spirit, and you are of two worlds longing for the home of forever and Him.

No matter your story before, this is your beginning now: you were formed by Love . . . for love.

John Calvin, he wrote it like a reviving breath—that

every human being is "formed to be a spectator of the created world and given eyes that he might be led to its author . . . first [to] cast our eyes upon the very beautiful fabric of the world in which [God] wishes to be seen by us. . . . As soon as we acknowledge God to be the supreme architect, who has erected the beauteous fabric of the universe, our minds must necessarily be ravished with wonder at His infinite goodness, wisdom and power."[1]

Ravished with wonder.

That the earth outside your window is tilted right now at just twenty-three degrees. So there are seasons and the vapors of oceans don't simply amass continents of ice, so the planet's bulk of six sextillion tons (that's twenty-one zeros) spins perfectly balanced on an invisible axis, spinning you around at one thousand miles an hour, nine million miles a year. Hurtling you through space even right now in this sun orbit at nineteen miles per second, 600 million miles a year. You, held in this moment by this unseen belt of gravity and turning these pages slowly while the miracle happens all around you: "He . . . poised the earth on nothingness" (Job 26:7, NJB).

Ravished with wonder.

Ravished by an even larger, bigger, more infinite Love.

So go to the window. Go to the hills, the desert, the

corner, the back door, and be ravished and taken and awed, and you who were made by Love, made for love—be still and know and watch love come down.

The answer to deep anxiety is the deep adoration of God.

And the greatest gift we can give our great God is to let His love make us glad.

Christmas begins here. The Christmas story, this love story—the whole blue marble of the world spinning right now on the Cross-beam axis of Love.

Unwrapping More of His Love in the World

What could you create today with a gentle heart of love (a letter, a treat, a surprise)? Create something out of your love!

We must be sure of the infinite good that is done to us by our Lord Jesus Christ, in order that we may be ravished in love with our God and inflamed with a right affection to obey Him, and keep ourselves strictly in awe of Him.

JOHN CALVIN

A Moment for Reflection

What in this whole blue marble of God's world causes you
to pause in wonder?

....

....

....

....

What does it mean to you that you were made out of the
overflow of God's love?

....

....

....

....

Think of three people who are not easy to love. What would
it look like to love those people with God's love?

....

....

....

....

They hid from the LORD God among the trees.

GENESIS 3:8

December 3

Where Are You?

Today's Reading

The woman . . . saw that the tree was beautiful and its fruit looked delicious, and she wanted the wisdom it would give her. So she took some of the fruit and ate it. Then she gave some to her husband, who was with her, and he ate it, too. At that moment their eyes were opened, and they suddenly felt shame at their nakedness. So they sewed fig leaves together to cover themselves.

When the cool evening breezes were blowing, the man and his wife heard the LORD God walking about in the garden. So they hid from the LORD God among the trees. Then the LORD God called to the man, "Where are you?"

GENESIS 3:6-9

For all the wandering, this is the first question of the Old Testament—God coming to ask after you, "Where are you?"

Where are you in your life? Where are you—from Me?

To get where you want to go, the first question you always have to answer is *Where am I?*

"Our fall was, has always been, and always will be, that we aren't satisfied in God and what He gives. We hunger for something more, something other."[2]

The only thing that will satisfy our hunger for more is to hunger for the One who comes down to Bethlehem, house of Bread, the One who comes after us and offers Himself as Bread for our starved souls.

And for all the wondering, this is the first question of the New Testament, when the wise men come asking, "Where is he?" (Matthew 2:2).

We only find out where we are when we find out where He is. We only find ourselves . . . *when we find Him.* We lost ourselves at one tree. And only find ourselves at another.

Wise men are only wise because they make their priority the seeking of Christ.

All our moments, all our waking—all the globe is a looking glass to God, and the wise keep seeking the presence of Christ in a thousand places, because you only come to yourself when you come to Him.

And your God, He's coming now, everywhere, for you. In all humanity's religions, man reaches after God. But in all His relationships, God reaches for man.

Reaches for you who have fallen and scraped your heart raw, for you who feel the shame of words that have snaked off your tongue and poisoned corners of your life, for you who keep trying to cover up pain with perfectionism.

Three words come through the dense thicket of failure: *Where are you?*

Your God refuses to give up on you.

Your God looks for you when you're feeling lost, and your God seeks you out when you're down, and your God calls for you when you feel cast aside. He doesn't run down the rebel. He doesn't strike down the sinner. He doesn't flog the failure.

Spurgeon writes that no matter what the day holds, how the season unfolds, God holds and enfolds: "I am come to find you wherever you may be. I will look for you till the eyes of My pity see you. I will follow you till the hands of My mercy reach you, and I will still hold you . . . to My heart."[3]

And that moment when your heart turns to His heart—already turned to you?

The Fall turns into a falling into His everlasting arms (Deuteronomy 33:27).

Unwrapping More of His Love in the World

Jesus is calling for you: "Where are you?" Sing a worship song or Christmas carol (or two or three), and invite Him to come and be with you.

When the year dies in preparation for the birth
Of other seasons, not the same, on the same earth,
Then saving and calamity go together make
The Advent gospel, telling how the heart will break.
Therefore it was in Advent that the Quest began.

C. S. LEWIS

A Moment for Reflection

What would you say if God called out to you now, "Where are you?"

What does it mean to you that God seeks you out and finds you when you are far from Him?

What places deep within your soul do you long for the Lord to seek out during this season of Advent?

Noah found favor with the LORD.

GENESIS 6:8

DECEMBER 4

Rise

Today's Reading

The LORD observed the extent of human wickedness on the earth, and he saw that everything they thought or imagined was consistently and totally evil. So the LORD was sorry he had ever made them and put them on the earth. It broke his heart. And the LORD said, "I will wipe this human race I have created from the face of the earth. Yes, and I will destroy every living thing— all the people, the large animals, the small animals that scurry along the ground, and even the birds of the sky. I am sorry I ever made them." But Noah found favor with the LORD.

GENESIS 6:5-8

In the midst of Advent, with the swags of cedar on porches and the lights twisted up streetlights, the headlines still spray across the face of the earth. They tear us open, and the world floods with pain. *God feels with us.* "His heart was filled with pain" (Genesis 6:6, NIV). God has a heart . . . *and it hurts. It hurts with what hurts us.* His heart hurts not just with a few drops of ache, not just with a slow drip of sadness—the whole expanse of His heart fills, swells, weighs dark with this storm of pain.

And God whispers close to us in a hurting world. A mother whose heart is bound to her child's? That doesn't compare to how your Father's heart is bound to you (Isaiah 49:15).

How did we ever find ourselves with the gift of finding favor with God?

God, who hung the stars—He has taken a thread of His heart and tied it to yours. And He didn't need to, but God tied His heart to yours so when you feel pain, He *fills* with pain.

"The tears of God are the meaning of history," writes American philosopher Nicholas Wolterstorff.[4] When sin effectively ended our time with God in the Garden, God could have effectively ended all time in the world.

But history and time still unfold—*gifts*—because God chooses tears.

The Flood was the flood of God's grief, and the essence of time is the tears of God.

Time only continues on in this impossibly suffering world *because God Himself is willing to keep suffering the impossible with us.*

While other creeds endeavor to get us out of the world and into heaven, in Christianity, heaven comes down and Christ comes into this world *to get us.* To suffer with us. We find favor—only because *Christ feels pain.*

Christ comes like an ark, like a cradle over floods. And we read the headlines and wonder, *If there's a God who really cares, He'd look at this world and His heart would break.*

And God looks to the Cross, that real Tree, and says, "My heart did."

On that Cross, they speared His side and pierced straight into His heart, filled with pain, and it was the water and blood of His broken heart that gushed right out, a flood of love.

It's the quantum physics of God: one broken heart always breaks God's in *two.*

God's heart breaks. Breaks in two—to let us into the ark of His love.

Every flood of stress is an invitation to get into the ark of our Savior.

Every flood of trouble remakes the topography of our souls—making us better or bitter.

Every trouble is a flood, and we can either rise up or sink down. And getting our days all into the ark of Christ always lets us still rise.

Grace—it, too, has floods of its own. . . .

The way heaven comes down so we can rise.

Unwrapping More of His Love in the World

Do one thing today just to please God.

Strange, this familiar Father of prodigals
whose love, too much for one lifetime,
wills that we shall share the
feast of forgiveness and joy
in the epilogue of eternity.

Strange, this daily advent of
EMMANUEL

J. F. WILSON

A Moment for Reflection

When have you felt flooded, overwhelmed by the waters rising around you?

....

....

....

....

In what ways has God been an ark in the midst of your own floods?

....

....

....

....

How does it feel to picture the tears of God, to know that He suffers alongside you?

....

....

....

....

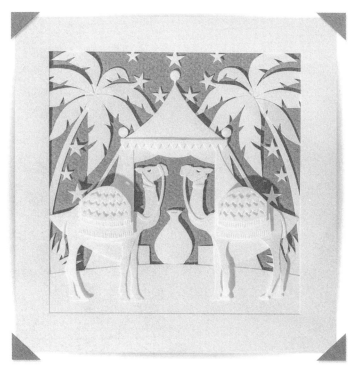

I will bless you . . . and you will be a blessing to others.

GENESIS 12:2

December 5

Living by Faith

Today's Reading

The LORD had said to Abram, "Leave your native
country, your relatives, and your father's family, and
go to the land that I will show you. I will make you
into a great nation. I will bless you . . . and you will
be a blessing to others. I will bless those who bless you
and curse those who treat you with contempt. All the
families on earth will be blessed through you."

So Abram departed as the LORD had instructed,
and Lot went with him. Abram was seventy-five years
old when he left Haran. He took his wife, Sarai, his
nephew Lot, and all his wealth—his livestock and
all the people he had taken into his household at
Haran—and headed for the land of Canaan. When
they arrived in Canaan, Abram traveled through the
land as far as Shechem. There he set up camp beside the
oak of Moreh. At that time, the area was inhabited by
Canaanites.

Then the LORD appeared to Abram and said, "I will
give this land to your descendants." And Abram built
an altar there and dedicated it to the LORD, who had
appeared to him.

GENESIS 12:1-7

This is the gift that wraps up all stresses quiet: *I will bless you.*

"I will bless you," says the God who comes to where you are. Who comes in the heaviness of the day, to the space where the weight hangs on the edges of you, so you just keep holding your breath, so you just keep forgetting to breathe.

But the weight of everything melts like thinning snow in the heat of His words: "I will bless you." He will not burden you. He will not break you. He will bless you— the God of invincible reliability, the God who has infinite resources, the God who is insistent love. You can always go ahead and breathe—He will bless. You can always breathe when you know all is grace.

That is the order of grace. . . .

The personal blessings envelop you first. Then you are the blessing sent to the world.

You will be experienced as a blessing—to the extent you have first experienced yourself as blessed. You must feel the fullness of your own pitcher before you trust the pouring out of yourself.

"It is no use for you to attempt to sow out of an empty basket, for that would be sowing nothing but wind," wrote Spurgeon.[5]

So slow down to feel the wind. Listen to the carols just a little bit longer. Linger in the quiet and taste the grace of now, and know that He is good and He is God. Name them in this moment—gift upon gift upon gift—and listen for the echo in everything: *I will bless you.*

D. L. Moody once wrote, "Faith is the gift of God. So is the air, but you have to breathe it; so is bread, but you have to eat it; so is water, but you have to drink it."[6]

Breathe it, eat it, drink it—leave the blur of Ur and slow to taste and see the promised land of Advent, of Christmas, of His Coming—the blessing of gift upon gift. Only when you first unwrap the gifts of blessings to you can you be wrapped up as a gift of blessing to others. Only when you are overwhelmed with the goodness of God can you overflow with the goodness of God to others.

And that is the blessing God graced Abram with, the blessing He graces you with this Advent, the gift that makes you a gift. The greatest gift God graces a soul with is His own presence.

So the whirl can hush and the spin can slow because He will bless, and He will bless with Himself come down. The present is His presence, and the greatest present you always have to give is His presence—looking into

41

someone's eyes as you listen, refusing the wrong of rushing, lingering long enough to really listen—to everything.

There is no need for more: the heart is full of gifts that is full of Christ.

It's strange how that happens—that any place becomes the Promised Land when the blessing of His presence becomes the gift we receive—and give.

Advent happening anywhere.

Unwrapping More of His Love in the World

Go to a new place today—to a neighbor's home you've never been before. Be a blessing and bring your neighbor a blessing of some sort. Leave him or her a Christmas card telling about Jesus, the blessing God gives to all people on earth!

The birth of the child into the darkness of the world made possible not just a new way of understanding life but a new way of living it.

FREDERICK BUECHNER

A Moment for Reflection

How has God blessed you, as He blessed Abram?

In what ways have other people overflowed God's grace into your life?

What are some ways you can be a blessing to others?

God has brought me laughter.

GENESIS 21:6

DECEMBER 6

Laugh!

Today's Reading

The LORD kept his word and did for Sarah exactly what he had promised. She became pregnant, and she gave birth to a son for Abraham in his old age. This happened at just the time God had said it would. And Abraham named their son Isaac. Eight days after Isaac was born, Abraham circumcised him as God had commanded. Abraham was 100 years old when Isaac was born.

And Sarah declared, "God has brought me laughter. All who hear about this will laugh with me. Who would have said to Abraham that Sarah would nurse a baby? Yet I have given Abraham a son in his old age!"

GENESIS 21:1-7

It happens just at the time God knew it would and should. You hear it in the middle of Advent, a whole string of notes that just come along and untie you: "Fa-la-la-la-la, la, la, la, la."

Notes like an echo of laughter.

Like children throwing back their heads and letting laughter, this oxygenated grace, cascade and cascade.

Like an old woman who cradles the unexpected, who cradles grace, who looks into the impossible made possible and laughs with the miraculous because that is what the relieved and re-livers do: "God has brought me laughter." You can almost see it—her wrinkles and weariness waning away, her lips cradling this smile.

God brings the weary woman laughter. Laughter is His gift—oxygenated grace.

"Joy, which was the small publicity of the pagan, is the gigantic secret of the Christian," writes G. K. Chesterton.[7]

The gigantic secret gift that He gives and we unwrap, that we never stop unwrapping—we who were barren now graced with the Child who lets us laugh with relief for all eternity. There is nothing left to want. There is nothing left to fear: "All fear is but the notion that God's love ends."[8] And His for you never will. So loosen up, because the chains have been loosed, and laugh the laughter of the freed. Laughter—it's all oxygenated grace.

In the press of a dark world, laughter comes to the Sarahs and the sufferers and the stressed as the reliever and then the reminder—that ache is not the last word for those who believe God. Jesus is. Jesus is the last word, and we rejoice and rejoice again and re-joy again because grace is our oxygen now.

"Angels can fly because they take themselves lightly," writes G. K. Chesterton.[9]

And somewhere a weary soul lets go of weight. And laughs thanks for the grace and takes more lightly—and it's like the sound of wings.

Like somewhere between heaven and earth, there is mirth—the echo of angels.

Unwrapping More of His Love in the World

Try keeping a smile on your face all day. Look for three opportunities today to make three different people laugh with you. We are the joy-filled people! We've been given the Son!

You have as much laughter as you have faith.

MARTIN LUTHER

A Moment for Reflection

When is the last time you laughed . . . really laughed?

What impossible thing are you longing for?

Like the angels, what can you take more lightly this Christmas?

Abraham called that place The LORD Will Provide.

GENESIS 22:14 (NIV)

DECEMBER 7

God Provides

Today's Reading

Some time later God tested Abraham. He said to him, "Abraham!"

"Here I am," he replied.

Then God said, "Take your son, your only son, whom you love—Isaac—and go to the region of Moriah. Sacrifice him there as a burnt offering on a mountain I will show you." . . .

Abraham took the wood for the burnt offering and placed it on his son Isaac, and he himself carried the fire and the knife. As the two of them went on together, Isaac spoke up and said to his father Abraham, "Father?"

"Yes, my son?" Abraham replied.

"The fire and wood are here," Isaac said, "but where is the lamb for the burnt offering?"

Abraham answered, "God himself will provide the lamb for the burnt offering, my son." And the two of them went on together.

When they reached the place God had told him about, Abraham built an altar there and arranged the wood on it. He bound his son Isaac and laid him on the altar, on top of the wood. Then he reached out his hand and took the knife to slay his son. But the angel of the LORD called out to him from heaven, "Abraham! Abraham!"

"Here I am," he replied.

"Do not lay a hand on the boy," he said. "Do not do anything to him. Now I know that you fear God, because you have not withheld from me your son, your only son."

Abraham looked up and there in a thicket he saw a ram caught by its horns. He went over and took the ram and sacrificed it as a burnt offering instead of his son. So Abraham called that place The LORD Will Provide.

GENESIS 22:1-2, 6-14 (NIV)

It is a thing: to call a place "The Lord Will Provide."

It is a thing to name where you live Provision, to name the place you call home "The Lord Will Provide."

To take your tired hand and turn the knob of that front door marked Provide and step right into the widening vista of Advent and find that the literal translation of "to provide" means "to see."

God always sees—and He will always see to it.

That is all that ever matters: God always sees, and He will always see to the matter.

Your legs may be weary and your heart may be heavy and your questions may be many, but whatever you are facing, it is always named Mount Moriah: the Lord will appear. The Lord sees. And He will see to it. And He will be seen.

The act of God's seeing means God acts. God's observing means He always serves. This is the thing: your God's constant vision is your constant provision.

You don't need to climb mountains named I Will Perform.

You don't need to climb mountains named I Will Produce.

Every mountain that every Christian ever faces, the Lord levels with sufficient grace: The Lord Will Provide.

This is what Abraham knows. You can see it in the way

he obeys unafraid and unquestioningly, the way he walks unhurried and unworried, the way he lives.

Worry is belief gone wrong. Because you don't believe that God will get it right.

Peace is belief that exhales.

Because you believe that God's provision is everywhere—like air.

In the thin air of Advent, you may not even know how to say it out loud: "I thought it would be easier." And your God comes near: *I will provide the way.* You may not even know who to tell: "I thought it would be different." And your God draws close: *I will provide grace for the gaps.* You may not even know how to find words for it: "I thought I would be . . . more." And your God reaches out: *I will provide Me.*

God gives God. That is the gift God always ultimately gives. Because nothing is greater and we have no greater need, God gives God. God gives God, and we only need to slow long enough to unwrap the greatest Gift with our time: time in His Word, time in His presence, time at His feet.

In this moment, in this middle of midwinter, in the dark of your very thickest thicket, there's the rough bark of the Tree. And there—you can feel it—the whitened wool of your willing Lamb. You can feel the willing pulse of His warm heart.

Advent is the time to see the Tree in your thicket and whisper the echoing words of your God: *Now I know. Now I know. Since You did not spare Your only Son, how will You not also graciously give us—even me—all things You know I need?* (Romans 8:32).

Now I know. Now I know, because You have not withheld from me Your Son, Your only Son. Now I know how You love me.

How He always has a ram in the thicket.

How He always provides—this bleating love calling you home.

Unwrapping More of His Love in the World

Write down ten different ways God has provided for you today, gift upon gift. Slip your piece of paper under your Jesse Tree. Thank God for being our Jehovah-jireh—in all ways.

Who can add to Christmas? The perfect motive is that God so loved the world. The perfect gift is that He gave His only Son. The only requirement is to believe in Him. The reward of faith is that you shall have everlasting life.

CORRIE TEN BOOM

A Moment for Reflection

When do you feel the pressure to perform, to produce?

Name the ways God has provided grace for the gaps in
your life.

Take a moment to thank God for the ultimate gift of salvation.

Surely the LORD is in this place, and I wasn't
even aware of it!
GENESIS 28:16

DECEMBER 8

The Stairway of God

Today's Reading

Jacob left Beersheba and traveled toward Haran. At sundown he arrived at a good place to set up camp and stopped there for the night. Jacob found a stone to rest his head against and lay down to sleep. As he slept, he dreamed of a stairway that reached from the earth up to heaven. And he saw the angels of God going up and down the stairway.

At the top of the stairway stood the Lord, and he said, "I am the Lord, the God of your grandfather Abraham, and the God of your father, Isaac. The ground you are lying on belongs to you. I am giving it to you and your descendants. Your descendants will be as numerous as the dust of the earth! They will spread out in all directions—to the west and the east, to the north and the south. And all the families of the earth will be blessed through you and your descendants. What's more, I am with you, and I will protect you wherever you go. One day I will bring you back to this land. I will not leave you until I have finished giving you everything I have promised you."

Then Jacob awoke from his sleep and said, "Surely the Lord is in this place, and I wasn't even aware of it!"

GENESIS 28:10-16

You can feel it in your bones sometimes when you stop for a moment—like life's this stairway that you just never stop climbing, this ladder that goes on forever without end.

Like all these lists are rungs, like your failures stretch from earth up to heaven, like all your rest feels like lying down on one unforgiving stone.

Sometimes you're just the most tired of trying to be strong.

You have these Jacob dreams, and you dream of what might be. And this is the dream that comes true—that makes all the stressed things come untrue: the real amazing dream is that there are no ladders to climb up, because Christ came down one to get you.

Jesus Christ Himself interprets the dream: "I tell you the truth, you will all see heaven open and the angels of God going up and down *on the Son of Man*, the one who is the stairway between heaven and earth" (John 1:51, emphasis added).

Jesus doesn't show you the steps to get to heaven—Jesus *is* the steps to heaven.

Jesus doesn't merely come down to show you the way up—Jesus comes down to make Himself into the Way to carry you up.

Jesus doesn't ultimately give you a how-to, because Christianity is ultimately about Who-to.

Every religion, every program, every self-help book is about steps you have to take. Jesus is the only One who becomes the step—*to take you.*

To take us who are the Jacobs, the dog tired and the debtors, the deluders and the desperadoes. To take us who are the lost and the long way from arriving, us who are bone weary of all the trying and the striving. Christ becomes the one step we can never take—and takes us. He comes to us like He comes to Jacob—He comes to us not in spite of our failings—but precisely because of them. Ours is the God who is drawn to those who feel down. Ours is the God who is attracted to those who feel abandoned. Ours is the God who is bound to those who feel broken.

Everywhere stairways for the sinners, everywhere ladders for the lost, everywhere gateways to God.

This is grace. This is reason to slow. This is not to be missed.

Why profane His coming with fleshly performances, frantic pushing, futile preoccupations?

Profanity, writes Elisabeth Elliot, is "treating as meaningless that which is freighted with meaning. Treating as common that which is hallowed. Regarding as a mere triviality what is really a divine design. Profanity is failure to see the inner mystery."[10]

We could slow and cease the profanity and see the inner mystery of here. Like our own rich variation of the Slow Food movement, we could begin the "Slow Christmas." We could set aside the to-do lists that profane the inner mysteries and slow to see the weight of glory in the moment at the sink—the divine design of a day that unfolds with a grace that is not to be missed. The hallowed here. Hurry always empties a soul . . . *slow*.

God doesn't want to number your failures or count your accomplishments as much as He wants you to have an encounter with Him.

The only ladder over you is Love—*and Love came down*.

If, just for a moment, you stand in the doorway, linger a bit in front of the tree, it's strange how you can see it—how every Christmas tree is a ladder and *Jesus* is your ladder who hung on that Tree . . . so you can have the gift of rest. When you are wrung out, that is the sign you've been reaching for rungs. The work at the very heart of salvation is the work of the very heart of Christmas: simply rest.

Here is holy.

The wonder of all this—God looks at you at your lowest and loves you all the way up to the sky.

Grace carries you all the way home.

Like heaven opening up slow everywhere.

Unwrapping More of His Love in the World

Love came down to help us in our helplessness. Today, find someone who is helpless and stoop low in love and service.

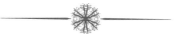

It is good to be children sometimes, and never better than at Christmas, when its mighty Founder was a child himself.

CHARLES DICKENS

A Moment for Reflection

When do you find yourself striving, reaching, grasping for the
next rung to try to pull yourself closer to God?

How would your perspective on the dailyness of life change
if you could see that here is holy?

Take a moment to thank Jesus for being your ladder to heaven
and to God.

You intended to harm me, but God intended
it all for good.

GENESIS 50:20

DECEMBER 9

Never Undone

Today's Reading

One day Jacob had a special gift made for Joseph—a
beautiful robe. But his brothers hated Joseph because
their father loved him more than the rest of them.
They couldn't say a kind word to him. . . .

The brothers killed a young goat and dipped Joseph's
robe in its blood. They sent the beautiful robe to their
father with this message: "Look at what we found.
Doesn't this robe belong to your son?"

Their father recognized it immediately. "Yes," he
said, "it is my son's robe. A wild animal must have
eaten him. Joseph has clearly been torn to pieces!" . . .

But now that their father was dead, Joseph's
brothers became fearful. "Now Joseph will show his
anger and pay us back for all the wrong we did to
him," they said.

So they sent this message to Joseph: "Before your
father died, he instructed us to say to you: 'Please
forgive your brothers for the great wrong they did to
you—for their sin in treating you so cruelly.' So we, the
servants of the God of your father, beg you to forgive
our sin." When Joseph received the message, he broke
down and wept. Then his brothers came and threw

themselves down before Joseph. "Look, we are your slaves!" they said.

But Joseph replied, "Don't be afraid of me. Am I God, that I can punish you? You intended to harm me, but God intended it all for good. He brought me to this position so I could save the lives of many people."

GENESIS 37:3-4, 31-33; 50:15-20

There's a storming mess this side of heaven.

There's this rising muck, and there's all of us.

And still there's this simultaneous global choreography that unfolds on the world stage anyway. . . .

String up a tangle of lights. Set a musty angel atop the tree. Deck the front porch and the back streets and the whole tilted world in this twinkling robe, this tinseled robe. Watch how it all spins in these lit colors.

Yet there is the robe's hem. There's always the bloodied, dirty dragging; there's always the ripped underside of things, the dreams and bits of us and unspoken hopes torn to pieces.

You can feel this—in a torn-up world, being torn apart.

When you are brave, you give yourself the gift of facing and touching the torn places. The places where we're torn to pieces can be thin places where we touch the peace of God.

Joseph touches his thin place. He feels along the edges of the torn places, and he sees through: "You intended to harm me, but God intended it all for good."

What was intended to tear you apart, God intends it to set you apart.

What has torn you, God makes a thin place to see glory.

Whatever happens, whatever unfolds, whatever unravels, you can never be undone.

You can stand around a Christmas tree with a family tree like Joseph's, with cheaters and beaters and deceivers, with a family like Jacob's, who ran away and ran around and ran folks down. But out of a family line that looks like a mess, God brings the Messiah. What was intended to harm, God intended all of it for good, and no matter what intends to harm you, God's arms have you. You can never be undone.

No matter what intends to harm you . . .

God is never absent,

never impotent,

never distant.

You can never be undone.

In the middle of all our collective mess stands the most monstrous evil. The wood of the crèche lies torn apart behind the wood of the Cross. The cries of the innocent Babe under the stars of Bethlehem twist into the agonized cries of the innocent Victim atop the injustice of Calvary. The holy dark over the manger gives way to the heinous dark over the Messiah and the slamming hammer and the tearing vein and the piercing thorn—the created murdering the Creator.

The Cross stands as the epitome of evil.

And God takes the greatest evil ever known to humanity and turns it into the greatest Gift you have ever known.

"If the worst things work for good to a believer, what shall the best things?" writes Puritan Thomas Watson. "Nothing hurts the godly . . . all things . . . shall co-operate for their good, that their crosses shall be turned into blessings."[11]

If God can transfigure the greatest evil into the greatest Gift, then He intends to turn whatever you're experiencing now into a gift. *You cannot be undone.*

Somewhere, Advent can storm and howl. And the world robed for Christmas can spin on.

You, there on the edge, whispering it, defiant through the torn places: "All is grace."

Unwrapping More of His Love in the World

Just as Joseph forgave his brothers, think of one person you can forgive today. Write down that person's name on a piece of paper. Then write out your thanks to God for taking that evil and making it good, for His promise that no matter what is done to you, He will not let you be undone.

A prison cell, in which one waits, hopes . . . and is completely dependent on the fact that the door of freedom has to be opened from the outside, is not a bad picture of Advent.

DIETRICH BONHOEFFER

A Moment for Reflection

When have you seen God take what was torn and turn it into a gift?

When have you seen God take what was torn and turn it into a gift?

What evils are you experiencing now that you need God to transform into something good?

In what areas of your life do you feel like you're coming unraveled? What would it feel like to have your heavenly Father slip a robe of righteousness over your shoulders?

[The Lord said,] "Oh, that their hearts would be inclined
to fear me and keep all my commands always, so that it
might go well with them and their children forever!"

DEUTERONOMY 5:29 (NIV)

Covenant of Love

Today's Reading

Moses summoned all Israel and said:

Hear, Israel, the decrees and laws I declare in your hearing today. Learn them and be sure to follow them. . . .

I stood between the LORD and you to declare to you the word of the LORD. . . . And he said:

"I am the LORD your God, who brought you out of Egypt, out of the land of slavery.

"You shall have no other gods before me.

"You shall not make for yourself an image in the form of anything in heaven above or on the earth beneath or in the waters below. . . .

"You shall not misuse the name of the LORD your God. . . .

"Observe the Sabbath day by keeping it holy. . . .

"Honor your father and your mother. . . .

"You shall not murder.

"You shall not commit adultery.

"You shall not steal.

"You shall not give false testimony against your neighbor.

"You shall not covet. . . ."

These are the commandments the LORD proclaimed in a loud voice to your whole assembly there on the mountain from out of the fire, the cloud and the deep darkness; and he added nothing more. Then he wrote them on two stone tablets and gave them to me. . . .

[The Lord said,] "Oh, that their hearts would be inclined to fear me and keep all my commands always, so that it might go well with them and their children forever!"

DEUTERONOMY 5:1, 5-22, 29 (NIV)

Love comes surely.

Like Advent and the Child, like night and the stars.

Like the gift of the Ten Commandments written with His very finger, this covenant to love.

They say that it came as a legal code, those Ten Commandments—but it is more. That it came as the inauguration of *shalom*, of the Kingdom—but it is more. Maybe this is the truest—that it comes as this whisper of His heart, your God entreating you to love.

Jewish weddings required a *chuppah*, a canopy covering, and your God comes down on Mount Sinai and gives the mountain a canopy of cloud. Jewish weddings required a *mikveh* so the bride could purify herself before the wedding, and your God gives the people before Mount Sinai time to purify themselves. And Jewish weddings required a *ketubah*, a contract for the loving, and your God gives these Ten Commandments for the living out of love.

The Ten Commandments are more than God saying, "Here is My Law for you"—they are God saying, "Here is My love for you."

Here, I take you to be Mine, to be My treasured possession—have no other gods, no other lovers that woo you, that take your attention or affection, but Me.

Here, I give you My name, my very name to make you mine—do not use it in vain.

Here, I long to spend time with you, holy time for you and Me—set apart the Sabbath day as holy time for you and Me.

Here, I love you, bride—be united, not coveting or lying or stealing or murdering or cheating one another, but honoring and loving and living out of our love.

And three times the Israelites say yes, this we will do— we do, we do, we do.

God gives His people this gift, these two tablets of stone with His handwritten commitment to love, and He aches. "Oh, that their hearts would be inclined to fear me and keep all my commands." *Oh, that their hearts . . . Oh, that*—this expression of unfulfilled longing in the Hebrew. God longs: "Oh, that your heart would obey me not because of Law, but because of love." God knows how we say I do—but don't. God longs that our hearts would be inclined to be in wonder and in awe of Me, enraptured by Me—that is what fear means in the original Hebrew. God knows how we say we wonder and we worship—but we don't.

God knows we wander, and He woos again and again, all through the commandments: "I am the Lord *Your* God, the Lord *Your* God, the Lord *Your* God." *You are mine. Make me Yours.*

Am I Yours?

God gives the Ten Commandments as more than Law—He gives them as a true commitment to love. God gives the Law—because He wants there to be love.

He gives his plea: "Oh, that you would obey Me—that's you giving Me love, and that's Me giving you love because this commandment to relationship fulfills your longings and your love and your being."

The Ten Commandments are a command to relationship.

To love vertically, to love horizontally, to love relationship—and it's not a suggestion.

Oh, that.

God's unfulfilled longing spills through time.

Till a voice echoes over Jerusalem: "O that at this time thou hadst known—yes even thou—what makes peace possible!" (Luke 19:42, WEY).

Jesus.

Jesus, the Love who seven days later went to the Cross to fulfill the unfulfilled, to pay the price for our broken love like we never could, to love God for His unbroken love like we never have.

Jesus, the Love who hangs on a Tree, who cries out our yes to the covenant: "My God, my God." Yes, You are mine. I am Yours. Yes, You are the Lord my God, the Lord my God, the Lord my God. Jesus, the Love who doesn't just die the death we deserved to die; He lives the love we've desired to live.

God gives the commandments to us—and God gives God to keep the commandments for us. God gives us the commitment of love at the top of Sinai, and He staggeringly keeps our commitment to love at the top of Calvary.

Who needs more than being loved to death?

"Love is the greatest thing God can give us, for himself is love," writes seventeenth-century theologian Jeremy Taylor. "And [love] is the greatest thing we can give to God, for it will also give ourselves. . . . The apostle calls [love] the bond of perfection. It is the old, and it is the new, and it is the great commandment, and it is all the commandments, for it is the fulfilling of the law."[12]

God gives God—and Jesus fulfills all the Law, all our love.

Stars will come in the night sky, shimmer somewhere. Advent will keep coming, this love story that never stops coming. Love like this could make us wonder. Somewhere, carols play.

They say that to this day Jews dance when the Ten Commandments are recited. Wooing love that makes the feet and the lights dance and the beloved weep.

Unwrapping More of His Love in the World

Find a quiet place to read the Ten Commandments, and as you do, dance before the Lord. Thank Jesus for amazing grace.

I am more sinful and flawed than I ever dared believe, more loved and welcomed than I ever dared hope.

ELYSE M. FITZPATRICK

A Moment for Reflection

Confess the ways you've broken God's commandments.

....

....

....

....

....

When have you felt afraid to approach God?

....

....

....

....

....

Write out your thanks to Jesus, whose love makes it possible
for you to approach a holy God.

....

....

....

....

....

You must leave this scarlet rope hanging from the window.

JOSHUA 2:18

December 11

A Scarlet Lifeline of Hope

Today's Reading

Joshua secretly sent out two spies from the Israelite camp at Acacia Grove. He instructed them, "Scout out the land on the other side of the Jordan River, especially around Jericho." So the two men set out and came to the house of a prostitute named Rahab and stayed there that night. . . .

Before the spies went to sleep that night, Rahab went up on the roof to talk with them.

"I know the LORD has given you this land," she told them. . . . "For the LORD your God is the supreme God of the heavens above and the earth below.

"Now swear to me by the LORD that you will be kind to me and my family since I have helped you. Give me some guarantee that when Jericho is conquered, you will let me live, along with my father and mother, my brothers and sisters, and all their families." . . .

Before they left, the men told her . . . "When we come into the land, you must leave this scarlet rope hanging from the window through which you let us down. And all your family members—your father, mother, brothers, and all your relatives—must be here inside the house. . . ."

"I accept your terms," she replied. And she sent them on their way, leaving the scarlet rope hanging from the window.

JOSHUA 2:1-21

There are swags and garlands and ribbons, and Advent gives away the Truth—we're all wishing for a lifeline.

We have deadlines. There's bumper-to-bumper traffic somewhere out on a freeway, a line of lights blinking tired in the dark. They're sticking a PICC line in a vein right now down at the cancer center. At the last gate at the end of the airport, folks wait in line with heavy bags in hand, just trying to get home.

And we trim the doorways with a line of links, these paper chains, as if Someone could be the Door and set us free.

Rahab has had a line waiting out her back door. Men lined up at her inn, wanting a place to lie down—and a piece of her. In a town with no Sabbaths, no lines of God's Word ever read, no prophets with a message of a coming visitation from heaven, she's one woman alone with the grime of too many nights on her hands, the weight of too many wounds on her heart—a woman who looks up in her godless mess and sees the tenderness of God. In a place of faithlessness and doubtfulness and godlessness, *God gives God.* The God who can reveal Himself wherever, whenever, to whomever; the God who is never limited by lack or restricted to the expected; the God who is no respecter of persons but the relentless rescuer of prodigals; the God who gives the gift of faith in the places you'd most doubt. That is always the secret to the abundant life: to believe that God is where you doubt He can be.

Rahab, in a godless place with a godless past, believes fully—and so lives fully. She steps out not in competence but in faith. She serves not her admirers but her adversaries. She saves the greatest gift for her family—a place of grace. She risks to live.

Rahab, the scarlet woman, flings a scarlet cord out her window—that one thread everything's hanging on. And that scarlet cord is her identity—that scarlet line running from the animal sacrifice covering Adam and Eve's nakedness in the Garden of Eden to the crimson markings of blood on the doorframes of the first Passover to the willing drops of blood in the garden of Gethsemane—and Rahab is delivered by that singular scarlet cord and tied into the Jewish family. And God makes the former woman of the night into a woman of the court—a princess and a wife of a Jewish prince, Salmon.

Their family line is furthered with a son—a son who would be the kinsman-redeemer of another foreign woman: a son named Boaz. The mother of Boaz is this Rahab; the mother-in-law of Ruth is this Rahab; the great-grandmother of the great King David is this Rahab. This Rahab, who is one of the women named in Scripture in the line that leads straight to this Jesus—that one thread everything's hanging on.

The great-grandmother of Christ many times removed—former prostitute, pagan, and profligate—Rahab finds herself the only other woman besides Sarah to be noted in the heroes' hall of faith. Rahab, right there beside the fathers of the faith—Abraham, Jacob, Isaac, Moses, and Noah: "By faith the harlot Rahab perished not with them that believed not, when she had received the spies with peace" (Hebrews 11:31, KJV).

Great faith is the greatest equalizer, the greatest eraser, and the greatest definer.

By faith, Rahab stands as "a blessed example both of the sovereignty of God's grace and of its power," writes the Puritan theologian John Owen. "Nobody, no sin, should lead to despair when the cure of God's sovereign, almighty grace is engaged."[13]

Nobody and no situation—no sin, no mess, no decision—meets the diagnosis of despair. Because there's God's cure of amazing grace.

No personal choice that muddied your life can ever trump the divine choice to wash your life clean.

No situation is more hopeless than your Savior is graceful.

That scarlet cord Rahab threw out that window?

In Hebrew, that cord is a *tikvah*.

The same word in Hebrew that means "hope."

You think about that as you tie string around Christmas gifts.

How strong a cord seems—until your life slips off the edge of a cliff and you lunge for something to hold on to.

One braid of fibers enough to hold you—that's your literal only hope.

You know it with startling clarity in that moment— how there's only a singular cord in this knotted mess of a world worth reaching for. It's dangling right there from our impossible tangle, and it's the one hope you need to reach for this Advent.

That scarlet lifeline of Christ.

Unwrapping More of His Love in the World

Do just one thing today that would be venturing big for God (share the gospel, make a hard phone call, do one thing you are scared to do but know Jesus is calling you to). Hold on to God, and do that one big thing by faith! Our God is bigger!

God is coming! God is coming! All the element we swim in, this existence, echoes ahead the advent. God is coming! Can you feel it?

WALTER WANGERIN JR.

A Moment for Reflection

Do you know what it's like to have a bad reputation? What does it mean to you that God's grace is enough to cover any kind of a past?

....

....

....

....

....

Rahab was remembered for her faith. What would you want to be remembered for?

....

....

....

....

....

Take time to thank Jesus for being your scarlet rope of salvation.

....

....

....

....

....

Your people will be my people, and your God
will be my God.

RUTH 1:16

December 12

Every Little Thing Is Going to Be Okay

Today's Reading

A severe famine came upon the land. So a man from Bethlehem in Judah left his home and went to live in the country of Moab, taking his wife and two sons with him. . . . Then Elimelech died, and Naomi was left with her two sons. . . . But about ten years later, both Mahlon and Kilion died. This left Naomi alone, without her two sons or her husband.

Then Naomi heard in Moab that the LORD had blessed his people in Judah by giving them good crops again. So Naomi and her daughters-in-law got ready to leave Moab to return to her homeland. . . .

But on the way, Naomi said to her two daughters-in-law, "Go back to your mothers' homes. . . ."

"No," they said. "We want to go with you to your people."

But Naomi replied, "Why should you go on with me? . . . Things are far more bitter for me than for you, because the LORD himself has raised his fist against me." . . .

But Ruth clung tightly to Naomi. "Look," Naomi said to her, "your sister-in-law has gone back to her people and to her gods. You should do the same."

But Ruth replied, "Don't ask me to leave you and turn back. Wherever you go, I will go; wherever you live, I will live. Your people will be my people, and your God will be my God. Wherever you die, I will die, and there I will be buried. May the LORD punish me severely if I allow anything but death to separate us!"

RUTH 1:1-17

There are Advent moments when you'd like nothing more than to order a Christmas miracle.

The one you need when it feels like no one really sees you. No one sees how alone you really feel. How overwhelmed by the work and unappreciated by the people. No one sees that you just want someone to cup your face and look into your eyes and say your name from somewhere deep inside, like a calling home, like a belonging—like a holding that has you around all the fragile places and won't leave you.

Some seasons are Naomi times. You ventured out with those hopes, full—and you feel you've been brought back empty . . . disillusioned, withered dry.

In some seasons, for all their gloss and glitz, it can be achingly hard to find gifts, and days can feel like fists.

Naomi—she goes home bitter. Orpah goes home to begin over. And Ruth goes on believing she will find home. Maybe sometimes the miracle begins by growing not in bitterness but in faithfulness—because, for all its supposed sophistication, cynicism is simplistic. In a fallen world, how profound is it to see the cracks? The radicals and the reflective, the Ruths and the revolutionaries—they are the ones on the road, in the fields, on the wall, pointing to the dawn of the new Kingdom coming, pointing to the light that breaks through all things broken, pointing to redemption always rising and the Advent coming again. Brilliant people don't deny the dark; they are the ones who never stop looking for His light in everything.

Ruth, who had given up her freedom for Naomi's future, who had gone with her back to that little town of Bethlehem—the outsider grafted in—she looks for His light, and she sees it: "Love is the face at the center of our universe. A sacred Smile; Holiness ready to die for intimacy."[14] But this can come too: expectations can come steal the gifts. Naomi, who has been given the gift of Ruth's sacrifice, sympathy, service—she's struggling to see it, to see the gift of the love still all around her. With her Ruth right there, clinging to her, she grieves: "I went away full, but the LORD has brought me home empty." It happens. When we have an agenda for God, we can't see the gifts from God.

There are no brazen miracles to be seen in the entire book of Ruth.

No angels appear stage left, no visions shatter the night, no heavenly hosts are overhead.

Much like the corner of Wallace and Main in the middle of December. Or like the annual family gathering at Aunt Muriel's with the embattled in-laws, the opinionated out-laws, the disinterested in-betweens. Or like your living room, your calendar, your day planner—all the mundane middle that just keeps pressing you in, stretching you out, deadening you slowly numb.

You know, like how Ruth just happens to end up in Bethlehem. Happens to end up gleaning in the field of about the only man who could be their kinsman-redeemer, Boaz—about the only one who has the right to buy back their lost ancestral land. Who just happens to meet her, hear her story, feel moved to offer to help. And she just happens to find him sleeping, follows her mother-in-law's instructions to ask him to spread his cloak over her—literally to "spread your wing over me," to save her from being preyed upon.

In Hebrew culture, she just proposed, asked him to take her—to marry her. She just said, "I want you to be my redeemer." And he just happens to say yes. And buys back the family land and redeems her and takes her and marries her, and together they happen to have a son. Named Obed. Which happens to mean "servant"—what union with your Redeemer always makes you. And Obed happens to have a son named Jesse, who has a son named David, who becomes the greatest king Israel has ever known.

Until David's line brings forth a King . . . named Jesus.

"The Holy Ghost thought fit to take particular notice of that marriage of Boaz with Ruth, whence sprang the Saviour of the world," writes Jonathan Edwards. "We may often observe it, that the Holy Spirit who indited the Scriptures, often takes notice of little things, or minute occurrences, that do but remotely relate to Jesus Christ."[15]

Every little thing is going to be okay because God is working good through every little thing.

All that's happening is happening to make miracles. The mundane is what's making miracles.

God comes through mangers. The mundane holds miracles. Every little thing *is* going to be okay—you have a Kinsman-Redeemer who takes you and is redeeming everything. The miracle of gifts is always unfolding under the impossibles.

"Joys are always on their way to us," assures Amy Carmichael. "They are always traveling to us through the darkness of the night. There is never a night when they are not coming."[16]

The miracle of gifts . . . is never not coming.

When your Father's hand isn't readily apparent, it's only because He's readying gifts. Gifts always come out of the unseen and hidden places.

It's a miracle itself—how you don't have to order a Christmas miracle. The miracle of Love is happening all around you.

Christ coming freely, willingly, now—coming unseen into everything.

Unwrapping More of His Love in the World

Write a card of thanks to someone in your church family today, or pick up the phone and give a lonely person a call. How can you be part of bringing a small miracle to someone in the family of God today?

The spirit of Christmas needs to be superseded by the Spirit of Christ. The spirit of Christmas is annual; the Spirit of Christ is eternal. The spirit of Christmas is sentimental; the Spirit of Christ is supernatural. The spirit of Christmas is a human product; the Spirit of Christ is a divine person. That makes all the difference in the world.

STUART BRISCOE

A Moment for Reflection

Like Naomi, do you sometimes miss the love all around you?
Name some of the people who have been faithful Ruths for you.

What little things eat away at you, worry you?

Your life may be devoid of brazen miracles, but God is at work
in the little things too. What events have "just so happened" to
come together in a way that indicates God is behind them?

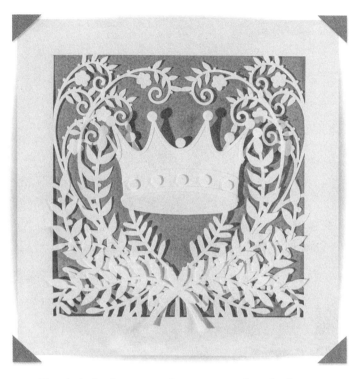

People judge by outward appearance, but the LORD looks at the heart.

1 SAMUEL 16:7

DECEMBER 13

Looking on Hearts

Today's Reading

The LORD said to Samuel . . . "Find a man named Jesse who lives there, for I have selected one of his sons to be my king. . . .

"Take a heifer with you," the LORD replied, "and say that you have come to make a sacrifice to the LORD. Invite Jesse to the sacrifice, and I will show you which of his sons to anoint for me."

So Samuel did as the LORD instructed. When he arrived at Bethlehem, the elders of the town came trembling to meet him. "What's wrong?" they asked. "Do you come in peace?"

"Yes," Samuel replied. "I have come to sacrifice to the LORD." . . .

When they arrived, Samuel took one look at Eliab and thought, "Surely this is the LORD's anointed!"

But the LORD said to Samuel, "Don't judge by his appearance or height, for I have rejected him. The LORD doesn't see things the way you see them. People judge by outward appearance, but the LORD looks at the heart."

Then Jesse told his son Abinadab to step forward and walk in front of Samuel. But Samuel said, "This is not the one the LORD has chosen." Next Jesse summoned Shimea, but Samuel said, "Neither is this the one the LORD has chosen." In the same way all seven of Jesse's sons were presented to Samuel. But Samuel said to Jesse, "The LORD has not chosen any of these." Then Samuel asked, "Are these all the sons you have?"

"There is still the youngest," Jesse replied. "But he's out in the fields watching the sheep and goats."

"Send for him at once," Samuel said. "We will not sit down to eat until he arrives."

So Jesse sent for him. He was dark and handsome, with beautiful eyes.

And the LORD said, "This is the one; anoint him."

1 SAMUEL 16:1-12

Advent reflects.

Candles flicker in windows, and you can see flamed light multiplied across dark. You can see your own face reflected in windowpanes, in a world of pain.

You can see it, too, how the world keeps looking for beauty in appearances rather than in His appearing.

Advent is this baptism of eyes.

Like a clear washing of eyes.

God tells Samuel that He has looked and He has found, provided for Himself a king. In Hebrew, God's literal words are "I've seen me a King."

"Looking comes first," is what C. S. Lewis writes in *The Great Divorce*.[17] Looking comes first if you're ever to find the life you want, if you are ever to "see you a king." Always, always—first the eyes. Joy is a function of gratitude, and gratitude is a function of perspective. You only begin to change your life when you begin to change the way you see.

Samuel—he sees the stature of Eliab and mutters, "Surely!" Surely this is the man in whom God's seen Him a king.

But the Lord draws near to Samuel: "The LORD doesn't see things the way you see them. People judge by outward appearance, but the LORD looks at the heart."

It's not just Samuel. It's us. It's the whole of humanity

who live fixated on facades, blinded to the realest real. The shiny shell of things can bind you and blind you. It's a veiled God who elevates the veiled things: the heart, the interior, the soul. And it's a temporal world that elevates the foil and the plastic, the status and the skills, the physical and the tangible—all this concrete mirage. Humanity obsesses with vapors, not eternity.

The reality is, you can lose your life, your joy if you are beguiled by the world's rind and blind to its inner reality. The endless bombardment of ads, gloss, Photoshop—it's like full-immersion sight lessons, schooling us to have eyes for everything unimportant and unreal. From Hollywood to Pinterest, the media of this world aggressively schools your soul to see the exact opposite of the way God sees.

People aren't bodies; they are hearts. We could train our eyes to turn everything inside out.

"Why should the eye be so lazy? Let us exercise the eye until it learns to see," writes G. K. Chesterton.[18] Let us exercise the eye until it sees through the fat of things, down to the eternal of things. Let us exercise the eye by walking with Christ.

There is this call for every Christian to answer His calling to be an ocular surgeon. Our seeing must cut through surfaces and down to souls.

You could close your eyes and ask it, see it. . . .

Is my life about the heart of things? Is my Christmas?

Am I deeply absorbed in Him and the heart of things? Or is my life a shallow absorption with surfaces?

It's strange how it affects us—from housekeeping to soul-keeping: if it's mostly the surfaces that absorb us, then we're mostly superficial. When my priorities aren't the things seen—when my priorities are rather all things unseen—it's only then that my life begins to have substance and weight.

Your God never stops turning things inside out, seeking all things unseen, reversing the ways of the world. God never stops looking on the heart. God never stops looking for the world's seconds, the unseen unimportant, and calls them the important firsts. Which means He raises Abel instead of Cain, Jacob instead of Esau, Isaac instead of Ishmael, Moses instead of Aaron, David instead of Eliab.

Which means He raises the unseen and forgotten: Sarah instead of Hagar, Leah instead of Rachel, Tamar, Hannah, Ruth, Rahab.

Which means that long after that unseen and forgotten son of Jesse was anointed king in Bethlehem, there was another unseen and unimportant One born in Bethlehem—One who was left out with the sheep because no one made room for Him either.

He who was the most beautiful One became the most ugly . . . that our ugly hearts might become beautiful in the eyes of God. Who knows of another love story like this?

The world—it seems different these few weeks of Advent. It *sees* different.

Each day of this Advent, we enter deeper into the story of Christ . . . and enter deeper into Him. And it's Him who gives us His eyes to really see.

To see past surfaces, to the heart of things—all the way down to the love.

Candles flicker in the window, reflected flames.

There is another forgotten One from Bethlehem—One who was not allowed in, who was kept out with the sheep and the animals. There was another who was anointed by the Spirit and sent out into the wilderness, not just hunted by Saul, but assaulted by Satan. There was another who was not just forgotten by his father, but forsaken by His Father. The most brilliant, beautiful Person in the universe lost his physical attraction (Isaiah 53) so that we, being spiritually unsightly, could be beautiful in the eyes of God.

Unwrapping More of His Love in the World

Seek out one person today who from the outside doesn't look like one of your friends. Take a few moments to sit down with that person and ask how his or her day is going. Look on the inside and lovingly listen to the heart.

O God and Father, I repent of my sinful preoccupation with visible things. The world has been too much with me. Thou hast been here and I knew it not. I have been blind to Thy presence. Open my eyes that I may behold Thee in and around me. For Christ's sake, Amen.

A. W. TOZER

A Moment for Reflection

When you look at other people today, how can you
concentrate on seeing hearts, not appearances?

What do you want to see with fresh eyes this Christmas?

Ask God to help your life be about the heart of things.

The people who walk in darkness will see a great light.

ISAIAH 9:2

Today's Reading

The people who walk in darkness
    will see a great light.
For those who live in a land of deep darkness,
    a light will shine. . . .

For a child is born to us,
    a son is given to us.
The government will rest on his shoulders.
    And he will be called:
Wonderful Counselor, Mighty God,
    Everlasting Father, Prince of Peace.
His government and its peace
    will never end.
He will rule with fairness and justice from the throne
      of his ancestor David
    for all eternity.
The passionate commitment of the LORD of Heaven's
      Armies
    will make this happen!

ISAIAH 9:2, 6-7

Light the Advent candles. Light them, light them.

Trim the wicks, watch the reflections, sit in the dark and wait.

Wait through the long, black night. Wait through the black that gets in your marrow. Wait through the dying, the cries you can't hear, the lurching gasp of the last death heaves. Sit through the night and the losses that scrape the sides of a soul, the burning tears that run, run through this night even now. Taste their saltiness and the darkness that seeps in cold at the corners and stains a thousand souls all alone.

Wait in the cosmic dark, inhale the black of an endless universe, stare into it and feel the darkness get darker.

"Our planet is a lonely speck in the great enveloping cosmic dark," wrote the American astronomer and astrophysicist Carl Sagan.[19]

That loneliness can envelop you in a loud room full of voices, when you stand at the window and watch the dusk thicken, when you turn out the last light.

To cross even the vast blackness of the Milky Way alone would take one hundred thousand years, traveling at the blurring speed of light. You turn this page under a roof, in a country, on a continent, near an ocean, on a planet—a pinpoint of a planet, a spinning orb waiting in the dark, waiting in the ache of Advent. You, this speck on a speck, floating in a ray of light, on a pale-blue dot suspended in the lonely blackness of space.

You can sit in the dark and feel the reverberating echo of Carl Sagan's words through our impossible emptiness, like a blaring headline for the world: "In our obscurity, in all this vastness, there is no hint that help will come from elsewhere to save us from ourselves."[20]

That is what one of our wise men decreed to us who are living, walking, dying in the darkness—that there's "no hint that help will come from elsewhere to save us from ourselves."

No hint of help. No rumor of relief. No sign of saving. For us waiting through the night, waiting through the dark.

And then . . . there it comes to the waiting, to the leaning, to the cold—a dawn! Light! Light!

Not mere candles wavering in the face of the black but a *dawn*—a dawn to crack back the black, to pry up the dark with bright shards, to peel it back and flood the cold room with light.

A light from beyond, erupting, heaving the black right back. A fire that the people walking in darkness did not set—but that they saw.

A light that the people in the dark couldn't ignite, couldn't inflame, and couldn't fabricate—but could only find.

Christmas can only be found.

Christmas cannot be bought. Christmas cannot be created. Christmas cannot be made by hand, lit up, set out, dreamed up. Christmas can only be *found*.

In the crèche. In the cradling trough. In the mire and in the stench and in the unexpected—and only in the dawning of Christ.

True, Mr. Sagan, there is no "hint" that help will come from somewhere else to save us. There is a dawn in the dark, there is unstoppable light, there is God-glory blazing.

Our God who breathes stars in the dark—He breathes Bethlehem's Star, then takes on lungs and breathes in stable air. We are saved from hopelessness because God came with infant fists and opened wide His hand to take the iron-sharp edge of our sins.

Our God who forms and delivers the black of the heavens—He waits patient like an embryo in a womb and delivers Himself to free you. We are saved from forever pain, because God pierced the dark and came to the pinpoint of us in the universe and took the nails.

Our God who cradles whole inking galaxies in the palm

of His hand, whom highest heavens cannot contain—He folds Himself into our skin, and He uncurls His newborn fingers in the cradle of a barn feeding trough . . . *and we are saved from ourselves.*

We are saved from our loneliness because God is love and He can't stand to leave us by ourselves, to ourselves.

That is the message of Christmas. The message of Christmas is not that we can make peace. Or that we can make love, make light, make gifts, or make this world save itself.

The message of Christmas is that this world's a mess and we can never save ourselves from ourselves and we need a Messiah.

For unto us a Child is born.

The Light never comes how you expect it. It comes as the unlikely and unexpected—straight into Bethlehem unlikely and the feed trough hopeless, and Christmas whispers there is always hope. It doesn't matter how dark the dark is; a light can still dawn. It doesn't matter if the world whispers, "There's not a hint that help will come from elsewhere," telling us that nothing will ever improve, get better, change. God favors the darkest places so you can see His light the brightest.

And once the light of Christ shatters your dark, shadows

forever flee your shadowlands. There's no going back and living in the dark; you live in the impenetrable, safe Light of light, and Christmas never ends for you. A Christian never stops living Christmas. True, you cannot light Christmas—*because it's Christmas that lights you*.

It's Christmas that dawns on you, and you only really believe in Christmas when you really live it. When you light a dark world and the unexpected places with a brave flame of joy; when you warm the cold, hopeless places with the daring joy that God is with us, God is for us, God is in us; when you are a wick to light hope in the dark—then you believe in Christmas. When you really believe in Christmas, you believe there is really hope for everyone. When you get Christmas, people get hope from you—they don't lose it.

Unless you keep passing on the miracle of hope, you live like Christmas is a myth.

So light the Advent candles. Light them, light them.

And you can see it, with every lit candle, sparks of the dawning.

Hope catching on everything.

Unwrapping More of His Love in the World

Bring someone a candle today and light it for him or her. Tell the person that you pray the light of Christ may warm his or her heart today. Fear not—don't hide His light under a bushel!

Late on a sleepy, star-spangled night, those angels peeled back the sky just like you would tear open a sparkling Christmas present. Then, with light and joy pouring out of Heaven like water through a broken dam, they began to shout and sing the message that baby Jesus had been born. The world had a Savior! The angels called it "Good News," and it was.

LARRY LIBBY

A Moment for Reflection

In what areas of your life do you need Christ's light to dawn?

Has your hope dimmed or flickered out somewhere along the way? Would you dare to ask God to reignite your hope again?

What is one thing you can do to spark hope for someone else today?

How much longer will you waver, hobbling between two opinions? If the LORD is God, follow him!

1 KINGS 18:21

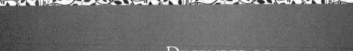

DECEMBER 15

Adore Him

Today's Reading

[Elijah said,] "You have refused to obey the commands of the LORD and have worshiped the images of Baal instead. Now summon all Israel to join me at Mount Carmel, along with the 450 prophets of Baal and the 400 prophets of Asherah who are supported by Jezebel."

So Ahab summoned all the people of Israel and the prophets to Mount Carmel. Then Elijah stood in front of them and said, "How much longer will you waver, hobbling between two opinions? If the LORD is God, follow him! But if Baal is God, then follow him!" But the people were completely silent.

Then Elijah said to them, "I am the only prophet of the LORD who is left, but Baal has 450 prophets. Now bring two bulls. The prophets of Baal may choose whichever one they wish and cut it into pieces and lay it on the wood of their altar, but without setting fire to it. I will prepare the other bull and lay it on the wood on the altar, but not set fire to it. Then call on the name of your god, and I will call on the name of the LORD. The god who answers by setting fire to the wood is the true God!" And all the people agreed.

1 KINGS 18:18-24

All of Advent, in the nave and the sanctuary, in the arching dome of a longing heart, it rises like a winding ribbon of incense: "Come, let us adore Him."

Let us leave the wrapping and the decking and the performing and come, awe at God.

Your hands need not bring anything of your own making. What God wants for Christmas is simply your bended knee.

They say that when you waver between two opinions, between two gods, the literal Hebrew word for wavering means *sinking.* It's our wavering between gods that has us sinking. It's the wavering between the gods of things and the God of everything—that's what has us flailing and drowning soundless in it all.

We were made to worship—our internal circuitry wired to worship. Every moment you live, you live bowed to something. And if you don't choose God, you'll bow down before something else—some banal Baal. Baal isn't the name of one particular god; it's the name of any generic god. Elijah confronted the people about their wavering, their sinking, between the God of Abraham and the Baal of rain. And for us, too, there are other Baals that can be our sinking. The Baal of success and the Baal of Pinterest, the Baal of perfection and the Baal of affirmation. It's always

Baals that keep us from God, the Baals of work and agenda and accomplishment that keep us from prayer. We don't pray enough only when we are practicing idol worship.

You can see how it goes—how there at the altars the Baal worshipers danced for rain. They strove and they flailed and they kept focused on trying to get all the steps just perfectly right—and that is how you ultimately know.

You know you have an idol whenever you have to perform.

You know you have a Baal that needs to be cut down whenever you cut yourself down. Whenever you slash yourself, you have an idol that needs to be slashed down.

Because that is what every idol ultimately wants: to make your blood run wild and dance you mad and drive you right into the unforgiving ground. Every idol wants you to be cut open for it.

But if you slow and still and wait, Advent whispers to you: there is one God who was cut open for you. He let His blood run so you can stop running. "The only way to overcome idols in your life," beckons Tim Keller, "is to see that Jesus gives you freely what every other god says that you can only get through your performance. Jesus gives you through His blood what every other god demands through yours."[21]

Jesus, the Gift, comes to *give* you freely through His passion what every other god forces you to *get* through your performance.

There in the nave, in the sanctuary, in the vaulting cathedral of your soul, you can hear how the notes come—one quaking, grateful note after another—as worship to the infant God who comes to the manger, the only God who comes to the wood on the altar, the God who takes the fire and who *is* the sacrifice to take you.

And you let everything go. And kneel. Kneel here and behold only Him—the only place where you can receive the gift of acceptance, so the gods of acceptance have no hold on you.

O come, let us adore Him . . .

The notes burning like a fire in the heart.

Unwrapping More of His Love in the World

Think of the Baals in your life—things you set your heart on besides the one true God. What is one thing you can do today to loosen the grip of one of those idols in your life?

Give me the Love that leads the way
The faith that nothing can dismay,
The hope no disappointments tire,
The passion that will burn like fire
Let me not sink to be a clod
Make me Thy fuel, Flame of God.

AMY CARMICHAEL

A Moment for Reflection

What emotions are evoked in you when you realize that God doesn't expect you to perform for Him—that He has already given you everything?

....

....

....

....

What sets God apart from every Baal, from every false god?

....

....

....

....

Set aside some time in the nave, in the sanctuary of your own heart, to come and adore Him.

....

....

....

....

....

Go . . . and deliver the message I have given you.

JONAH 3:2

The Gift of the Storm

Today's Reading

The LORD gave this message to Jonah son of Amittai: "Get up and go to the great city of Nineveh. Announce my judgment against it because I have seen how wicked its people are."

But Jonah got up and went in the opposite direction to get away from the LORD. He went down to the port of Joppa, where he found a ship leaving for Tarshish. He bought a ticket and went on board, hoping to escape from the LORD by sailing to Tarshish. . . .

Now the LORD had arranged for a great fish to swallow Jonah. And Jonah was inside the fish for three days and three nights. . . .

Then the LORD ordered the fish to spit Jonah out onto the beach.

The LORD spoke to Jonah a second time: "Get up and go to the great city of Nineveh, and deliver the message I have given you."

This time Jonah obeyed the LORD's command and went to Nineveh, a city so large that it took three days to see it all. On the day Jonah entered the city, he shouted to the crowds: "Forty days from now Nineveh will be destroyed!" The people of Nineveh believed

God's message, and from the greatest to the least, they declared a fast and put on burlap to show their sorrow.

JONAH 1:1-3, 17; 2:10; 3:1-5

Storms track across the radars.

Snow falls on cedars somewhere up in the mountains, piles of white weighing down pines.

Clouds keep churning out on the ocean and up the battered coasts and along the ragged edges of you. Escape can seem alluring.

Advent can feel like an advent of crises. A whole string of Jonah-days brazenly begging you to head in the opposite direction, to get away from the dark underbelly of people and agendas and loving the unlovely and loud. Jonah finds a boat and buys a one-way ticket and sails due west, as if a man can ever escape the grace of God. As if finding your ship isn't sometimes more like jumping ship.

A storm meets Jonah head-on in his.

It shakes the drowsing man awake—God's coming, His Advent, always shakes us to awake. And it cups hold of Jonah's wet, disoriented face and flat out startles him with the gift of utter dependence. Jonah-days chase you for tender reason. The Hound of Heaven storms after you till you have the gift you need.

You aren't equipped for life until you realize you aren't equipped for life. You aren't equipped for life until you're in need of *grace*.

In the moment of realizing your limitations, your shortcomings, your inescapable sins, all that you aren't—in that moment of surrendered lack, you're given the gift you'd receive no other way: the gracious hand of an unlimited God. Repentance, turning around, is the only way to be ushered into grace.

Jonah turns from his running, owns his own complicity, sacrifices himself off the edge of the boat to save his boat mates. He descends the depths and tosses and turns three days in the curdling, churning belly of the fish before being heaved up alive on dry land.

Then he turns back. Turns back to God, turns back to Nineveh to plead with them, with everybody, to just turn back.

"We all want progress," writes C. S. Lewis. But "if you are on the wrong road, progress means doing an about-turn and walking back to the right road; and in that case, the man who turns back soonest is the most progressive."[22]

She who turns back soonest is the most progressive. She who repents most makes the most progress—you always go farther when traveling light. She who repents of seemingly little sins knows that all sins are great—and knows a greater God. Repentance is as much air to a Christ-follower as faith.

Nearly eight hundred years after Jonah, another Man boards a boat and sleeps through a great storm. He awakens to anxious boat mates. He calms the storm—not by owning His complicity but by taking on ours. He assures,

"One greater than Jonah is here" (Matthew 14:21). Because He doesn't calm one storm but all storms. He casts Himself into our waves, into our storms, into our depths; He sacrifices Himself for our saving; and He is binding the broken and raising the dead and re-membering you. Jonah was three days and three nights in the belly of the great fish, but Jesus took three days and three nights in the heart of the earth, in the belly of death, *so no one else would ever have to.*

He did not abandon you in the ultimate storm of your soul. He will not abandon you in the immediate storm of your now.

He asks you, calls you, begs you to believe. Will you believe the wild miracle of a storm and a resurrection from the belly of a fish? Will you believe the wilder miracle of the Word made flesh, God with skin, God in a trough, God on a Cross? Will you believe in your own resurrection from the belly of sin? Will you believe in miracles? You can whisper that word *repentance*—and find yourself resurrecting. Turning around and resurrecting.

There's snow falling heavy over a cabin tucked under pine trees right now. Storms could get worse in the north today. Or closer.

Advent never stops coming for you.

Turn around and watch it come. Just slow and turn around.

Unwrapping More of His Love in the World

Write down one thing you repent of today. Draw a heart around it. Tuck it under the Jesse Tree as your gift to Jesus of a contrite heart, and pray that Jesus would help you give up this sin.

[Advent] is a time of quiet anticipation. If Christ is going to come again into our hearts, there must be repentance. Without repentance, our hearts will be so full of worldly things that there will be "no room in the inn" for Christ to be born again. . . . We have the joy not of celebration, which is the joy of Christmas, but the joy of anticipation.

JOHN R. BROKHOFF

A Moment for Reflection

When have you found yourself running from God? How did He draw you back to Himself?

In what ways have you seen God calm the storms in your life?

Thank God that He invites you to turn around, to be resurrected.

You, O Bethlehem Ephrathah, are only a small village.

MICAH 5:2

Lifting Up the Little and Small

Today's Reading

You, O Bethlehem Ephrathah,
    are only a small village among all the people
      of Judah.
Yet a ruler of Israel,
    whose origins are from the distant past,
    will come from you on my behalf.
The people of Israel will be abandoned to their enemies
    until the woman in labor gives birth.
Then at last his fellow countrymen
    will return from exile to their own land.
And he will stand to lead his flock with the LORD's
      strength,
    in the majesty of the name of the LORD his God.
Then his people will live there undisturbed,
    for he will be highly honored around the world.
    And he will be the source of peace.

MICAH 5:2-5

O little town of Bethlehem Ephrathah and Scappoose, Oregon, and Wallagrass, Maine, and Americus, Kansas, and the quiet side streets and living rooms of a million small and unlikely places—Kingdom comes to places like you.

You, there, with your lights strung up and down like sequins that have seen better days. With your ragamuffin kids and paint-chipped Christmas ornaments from 1982, your scarlet poinsettias in the front window, in the fading light of the front room.

There's a winter wonderland set up on someone's mantel. They'll get carolers to come round to the nursing home this Friday night and sing, "Hark! the herald angels sing / Glory to the newborn King." Everyone will smile worn and grateful, and no one will care if it's off key.

Because there is a king in Bethlehem. In backwater Bethlehem, an unmarried hardly-woman in labor giving birth to your King, and He will be your newborn and ancient and coming and future King, newly birthed, whose goings-forth have been from of old, from ancient days. A King like and infinitely greater than King Arthur, with his tomb inscription: *"Hic iacet Arthurus, rex quondam, rexque futurus"*—"Here lies Arthur, king once, and king to be." Forsake the fairy tales for the story that is history: *this*

Bethlehem King is the true and the real once and still coming King—the King of humanity's memory. The King from the beginning, back when we were young and the world was Edenic and the wonderland was us.

There's your winter wonderland set up on the cosmic stage: the Son is sent in through the fallen kingdom's back door, the King is born into a barn to wrest the forces from the pit, slay the demons, crush the head of the evil one, and woo the world back to life. The war is bloody. It is heinously dark. And on Calvary, evil corners the Son. Iron spikes the King to a Tree and laughs haunting triumph—only to have light shatter the dark and the King fling off the rotting grave clothes and rise.

Author J. R. R. Tolkien called this moment when the light of deliverance throws back the darkness the "eucatastrophe"—the moment when evil is dashed and righteousness suddenly, spectacularly rises.

"The Birth of Christ is the eucatastrophe of Man's history," writes Tolkien. The birth of the King is the light in your story, in history, that slashes back the smothering dark. The birth of Christ is, for the band of survivors, the saved hushed there in the manger of Bethlehem, the moment of eucatastrophe, of joy—that "catch of the breath, a beat and lifting of the heart." In that eucatastrophe instant, under a Bethlehem star when humanity witnesses the King-God inhale earth air into His lungs, you can feel it: "joy beyond the walls of the world."[23]

Because the King beyond this world has entered this world, and the wonderland in Him we always hoped for is here and now and true.

The unexpected Bethlehem King is the once and coming King, the King of the first and still coming second Advent, the King coming again to rule the earth and make all the sad things untrue.[24] The wonderland is unfolding even now, Kingdom coming, because His Word "will not return to me empty, but will accomplish what I desire and achieve the purpose for which I sent it. You will go out in joy and be led forth in peace; the mountains and hills will burst into song before you, and all the trees of the field will clap their hands" (Isaiah 55:11-12, NIV).

The dance of the sugarplum fairies just withered a bit.

The very trees of the fields are going to dance and clap their hands. The King is coming, and the new Kingdom is stirring. And stirring in you. When the King rules your world, you cease to rule or worry. All worry dethrones God. All worrying makes you King and God incompetent.

There is a King born in Bethlehem and on the throne. You can breathe.

There are Christmas trees blinking in living rooms tonight in Americus, Kansas, and Quitman, Arkansas, and Mud Lake, Idaho.

Someone plays it on a piano that needs tuned: "Glorrrry to the newborn King."

And in small towns and in the little town of Bethlehem, the lights on all the trees dance.

For the coming King, the trees of the field all dance.

Unwrapping More of His Love in the World

Look for someone today who is doing some little, good thing that is likely to go unnoticed. Slip that person a happy note to say he or she is making a difference!

It was not suddenly and unannounced that Jesus came into the world. He came into a world that had been prepared for Him. The whole Old Testament is the story of a special preparation. . . . Only when all was ready, only in the fullness of His time, did Jesus come.

PHILLIPS BROOKS

A Moment for Reflection

When have you felt like Bethlehem . . . poor, small, forgotten?

What worries do you need to surrender to God, knowing He is firmly on His throne?

Take a moment to thank God for the eucatastrophe of Christmas—for conquering evil with righteousness.

I will go in to see the king.

ESTHER 4:16

DECEMBER 18

Come to the King

Today's Reading

Esther told Hathach to go back and relay this message to Mordecai: "All the king's officials and even the people in the provinces know that anyone who appears before the king in his inner court without being invited is doomed to die unless the king holds out his gold scepter. And the king has not called for me to come to him for thirty days." So Hathach gave Esther's message to Mordecai.

Mordecai sent this reply to Esther: "Don't think for a moment that because you're in the palace you will escape when all other Jews are killed. If you keep quiet at a time like this, deliverance and relief for the Jews will arise from some other place, but you and your relatives will die. Who knows if perhaps you were made queen for just such a time as this?"

Then Esther sent this reply to Mordecai: "Go and gather together all the Jews of Susa and fast for me. Do not eat or drink for three days, night or day. My maids and I will do the same. And then, though it is against the law, I will go in to see the king. If I must die, I must die." So Mordecai went away and did everything as Esther had ordered him.

ESTHER 4:10-17

Sometimes you see them huddling under the bridge on the west side. Two or three of them, their hats pulled wind thin over their ears. They look like hungry prayers, their bare hands held out over flame licking off the sides of an old oil barrel.

So much for chestnuts roasting on the open fire.

This is about the open fire warming the tips of your numbed fingers, distracting you from the cold icing down the nape of your neck.

How does Advent come and kindle in the guy living out of a cardboard box behind the busy mall in mid-December? In the woman slapped around in the flat over the bar serving up office Christmas parties? In the pregnant runaway down at the bus station who's watching everybody head home and doesn't know where the next meal will come from, the next kind word, the next clean bed?

Mordecai—he was in sackcloth outside the palace gate.

He sent word to his niece, chosen queen of the king, to never forget the plight of those collected on the other side of the gate: "Don't think for a moment that because you're in the palace you will escape when all other Jews are killed. If you keep quiet at a time like this, deliverance and relief for the Jews will arise from some other place, but you and your relatives will die."

It comes like a whisper from those outside the gate: *You've got to use the life you've been given to give others life.*

You've got gifts that weren't given to line your life with; they were given to be a lifeline to others—or you lose your life.

It comes like an echo from God: if your gifts don't give relief, you don't get real life.

What does it profit a man to gain the whole world but lose his own soul?

It comes as a message for Advent, the Mordecai message for such a time as now: you've got to use your position inside the gate for those outside the gate—or you're in the position of losing everything.

If you have any food in your fridge, any clothes in your closet, any small roof, rented or owned, over your head, you are richer than 75 percent of the world. We are the ones living inside the gate.

If you have anything saved in the bank, any bills in your wallet, any spare change in a jar, you are one of the top 8 percent wealthiest people in the world. We are the ones living inside the gate.

If you can read these words right now, you have a gift three billion people right now don't. If your stomach isn't twisted in hunger pangs, you have a gift that one billion people right now don't. If you know Christ as the greatest Gift, you have a gift that untold millions of people right now don't. *We are the ones living inside the gate.*

Esther hears the Mordecai message, and it does something to her soul. *You've got to use your position inside the gate for those outside the gate—or you're in the position of losing everything.*

Esther puts herself in the place of those outside the gate and makes herself the bridge to the King. And the woman given gifts for such a time as this—she risks her position for the people. *If I perish, I perish.*

There's a boy right now splayed in the slum and sewage of Calcutta. A child crying weak for food in Uganda, this haunting plea like the cry of the last raven. And there's One whose home was the original palace, One who is the apex of beauty, One who put Himself in the place of you outside the gate, you in the muck and the mire and the stench of sin. There is One who came to a barn and made Himself a bridge back to the King by laying down His back on the bark of that Tree. He looked at you desperate on the outside of the gate, and His love was instant. He didn't ponder, *If I perish, I perish.* He promised, "So I perish, I perish."

This is the love story that has been coming for you since the beginning. That Babe in the manger—He is the Prince on the Cross who saves you with His life, so your identity is no longer wrapped up in being one of the rich ones inside the gate. Your identity is wrapped up in being one of the rich ones *inside of Him.*

When you unwrap your worth in the Gift of Christ, you release your grip on all the other gifts. You are loved and carried and secure, and what else do you need when you have Him? You are free, *free*, to lavishly give away your gifts when all your value, worth, joy, and riches are in the greatest of gifts.

Why, writes George Müller, would anyone inside the gate "seek to be rich, and great, and honored in that world where his Lord was poor, and mean, and despised"?[25]

You can see it during Advent—over on the west side, over in the slum, over the backyard fence—the way someone reaches out a hand and someone weak grabs hold. And all the gates give way to God.

For such a time as this.

Unwrapping More of His Love in the World

God made you for such a time as this. Find one person you can help today in a time of need.

Enemy-occupied territory—that is what this world is. Christianity is the story of how the rightful king has landed . . . and is calling us all to take part in a great campaign of sabotage.

C. S. LEWIS

A Moment for Reflection

What specific gifts has God given you?

As you look at those "outside the gate," who do you feel especially drawn to help?

How might you use some of your gifts to help others—for such a time as this?

I will climb up to my watchtower and stand at my guardpost. There I will wait to see what the Lord says.

HABAKKUK 2:1

DECEMBER 19

Watching for Him Who Is Enough

Today's Reading

I will climb up to my watchtower
   and stand at my guardpost.
There I will wait to see what the LORD says
   and how he will answer my complaint. . . .

I trembled inside when I heard this;
   my lips quivered with fear.
My legs gave way beneath me,
   and I shook in terror.
I will wait quietly for the coming day
   when disaster will strike the people who invade us.
Even though the fig trees have no blossoms,
   and there are no grapes on the vines;
even though the olive crop fails,
   and the fields lie empty and barren;
even though the flocks die in the fields,
   and the cattle barns are empty,
yet I will rejoice in the LORD!
   I will be joyful in the God of my salvation!
The Sovereign LORD is my strength!
   He makes me as surefooted as a deer,
   able to tread upon the heights.

HABAKKUK 2:1; 3:16-19

There are Christmas trees that have no blossoms.

There are a thousand ways you can suffer brave.

And no one knows.

No one knows that, like Habakkuk, your heart quakes a bit inside. At how headlines hit too close, how in a blink on an ordinary day, it could be one you love who is bloodied by the senseless violence, busted in a crash, begging prayers for life, getting chemo pumped through the veins. We all lose every single person we love. There is never another way. Think about that too long and you find it hard to breathe.

The economy crumbles away under your feet. If one more thing breaks down, if one medical disaster pushes you over the fragile edge, what in the world do you grab on to in this mudslide of debt? Fear is always this wild flee ahead.

Olives fail. People fail. Dreams fail. *You feel like you fail.* A thousand things mount. Some days it's hard not to panic. You can feel it—we are driven by fear of failure. For all our frenzied running around, could it be that we are actually fleeing— trying to escape all the fears? All this pain? All this failure? We all live these lives of quiet terror. Of soundless, hidden grief. You could just bow your head in the quiet and weep for all that isn't. For all that you aren't.

In the barrenness of winter, Habakkuk offers this gift to

always carry close: rejoicing in the Lord happens while we still struggle in the now.

Struggling and rejoicing are not two chronological steps, one following the other, but two concurrent movements, one fluid with the other.

As the cold can move you deeper toward the fire, struggling can move you deeper toward God, who warms you with joy. Struggling can deepen joy.

Even though.

Even now.

Even though the fig trees have no blossoms and though the Christmas tree aches a bit empty, even though there are no grapes on the vine and no struggle-free days, even though the olive crop fails, even though I fail, even though *so much fails*— even now I will rejoice in the Lord.

Even now I will be joyful in the God of my salvation.

Even though, even now—Habakkuk turns the focus. The secret of joy is always a matter of focus: a resolute focusing on the Father, not on the fears. All fear is but the notion that God's love ends. *When does He ever end?* When you can't touch bottom is when you touch the depths of God.

Habakkuk rings it again defiant from the watchtower into a struggling world—I will be joyful in the God of my salvation. Re-joys, re-joices, and again. Soon the angels will sing it: "Fear not! For behold!" The solution to fear is the gift of Christmas. "Fear not! For behold!" We have a Savior. "Since he did not spare even his own Son but gave him up for us all, won't he also give us everything else?" (Romans 8:32). He shattered the space between heaven and earth and came naked and breakable for you in a crèche. Then He lay naked and broken by you on a Cross. If He gave you His Son to save you, will He not give anything?

Hasn't He already unequivocally earned trust? You can take your hands off your life—you don't have to try to save yourself. Behold Him everywhere, and be held.

Though the fig tree does not blossom, *His love always does.*

Instead of explaining our struggling, *Jesus shares in it*— because He knows mere answers are cold and His arms are warm.

The watchtower can be climbed. Stand even now at the guardpost; there are gifts.

Count, recount gifts: rejoice, re-joice. Our worlds reel unless we rejoice. A song of thanks steadies everything.

Behold the goodness of the God of your salvation everywhere, and be held—how His love falls like blossoms of grace in December.

Unwrapping More of His Love in the World

Take time today to climb your watchtower. In those moments of quiet, reflect on the joys you've been given— and then repeat them.

Assurance grows by repeated conflict. . . . When we have been brought very low and helped, sorely wounded and healed, cast down and raised again . . . and when these things have been repeated to us and in us a thousand times over, we begin to learn to trust simply to the word and power of God.

JOHN NEWTON

A Moment for Reflection

What are you waiting on God for right now?

Where have you seen blossoms of goodness even in the most unlikely places?

Thank God for the grace to rejoice amid the broken places.

He will prepare the people for the coming of the Lord.

LUKE 1:17

DECEMBER 20

When All the Miracles Begin

Today's Reading

Zechariah and Elizabeth were righteous in God's eyes,
careful to obey all of the Lord's commandments and
regulations. They had no children because Elizabeth
was unable to conceive, and they were both very old.

One day Zechariah was serving God in the Temple,
for his order was on duty that week. As was the
custom of the priests, he was chosen by lot to enter
the sanctuary of the Lord and burn incense. While the
incense was being burned, a great crowd stood outside,
praying.

While Zechariah was in the sanctuary, an angel
of the Lord appeared to him, standing to the right
of the incense altar. Zechariah was shaken and
overwhelmed with fear when he saw him. But the
angel said, "Don't be afraid, Zechariah! God has heard
your prayer. Your wife, Elizabeth, will give you a son,
and you are to name him John. You will have great
joy and gladness, and many will rejoice at his birth,
for he will be great in the eyes of the Lord. He must
never touch wine or other alcoholic drinks. He will be
filled with the Holy Spirit, even before his birth. And
he will turn many Israelites to the Lord their God. He

will be a man with the spirit and power of Elijah. He will prepare the people for the coming of the Lord. He will turn the hearts of the fathers to their children, and he will cause those who are rebellious to accept the wisdom of the godly."

LUKE 1:6-17

It's the time when all the miracles begin.

God has been silent for four hundred years.

After He spoke to the prophet Malachi, the Old Testament falls mute. It's been four long, neck-straining centuries where you could look up to heaven . . . and hear a pin drop.

Tears drop.

No one has glimpsed an angel for at least half a millennium. It has been six hundred years since Shadrach, Meshach, and Abednego cut through the flames of the furnace with a fourth blinding torch from heaven. Eight hundred years have slow-dripped by since Elijah and Elisha and that bygone era of miracles. When we're blind to grace, is the miracle we get that we get homesick for Him?

Then, in a prayer and a blink, four hundred years shatter. The volume of God reverberates in hearts, and the strobes of heaven dance.

Angel glory appears in front of one old man. A certain wrinkled and graying priest. Not a particularly notable one—just one of a sea of eighteen thousand. One priest who's awestruck that his name has been drawn to offer the incense in the Holy of Holies on the once-a-year Day of Atonement. Throughout the whole of a priest's life, his name might never be drawn. And once it was, it could never be drawn again.

Zechariah breathes through the miracle of his priest-hood—one man named "God Remembers," an undistin-guished old man without a son to pass down the priesthood, married to one time-engraved woman named "My God Is an Oath." A woman ashamed and disgraced at the barren-ness of oaths. God bends His heart to hear the prayer of the breaking—the remembering God of the small and the forgotten—and miracles begin again here.

Miracles begin understated. They begin, and the earth doesn't shake and trumpets don't sound. Miracles begin with the plainsong of a promise—and sometimes not even fully believed. This is always the best place for miracles: God meets us right where we don't believe. When our believing runs out, God's loving runs on.

This is the season of the Advent of God. The barren will birth. Dreams will wake into reality. Nothing is impossible with God.

That's what the angel plainly assures: "God Remembers" and "My God Is an Oath" will birth "God Is Gracious." The miracle always is that God is gracious, that grace carries us and breathes life into the dead and impossible places, that grace—a thousand graces—explodes the doubt-ing silence in our hearts.

Zechariah has doubt. He struggles with the doubts, can't

silence the questions. Not unlike Mary, with doubts and questions of her own. Yet Zechariah finds himself struck dumb—and Mary finds herself God-struck with blessings.

There is this. Never doubt that there are two kinds of doubt: one that fully lives into the questions, and one that uses the questions as weapons against fully living.

Breathe easy into the questions. The name of God, *YHWH*—inhale, exhale—is the sound of your breathing. There is your miraculous answer. As long as you are breathing, He is always your miraculous answer.

The angel breathes a word from the Lord about the front-runner of the Lord: "He will be a man with the spirit and power of Elijah." The era of miracles is here! "He will prepare the people for the coming of the Lord."

And *He* will prepare your heart for the coming of the Lord. Now the miracles stack, multiply. You don't have to work for the coming of the Lord—you don't have to work for Christmas. *The miracle is always that God is gracious.* You don't have to earn Christmas, you don't have to perform Christmas, you don't have to make Christmas. You can rest in Christ. You can wait with Christ. You can breathe easy in Christ. Open your heart to the miracle of grace. *He* will prepare your heart for the coming of the Lord.

"This is the true preparedness of heart for coming to Christ, the preparedness of coming to him just as you are," Charles Spurgeon wrote.[26]

Your name has been drawn. Come to Him just as you are. Give up trying to be self-made: this is your gift to Him—and His gift to you. *Simply come.* The miracle of Christmas is that you get more than proof of God's existence. You get the experience of God's presence.

You always get your Christmas miracle. You get God with you.

God gives God. He withholds no good thing from you.

And the good things in life are not so much health, but holiness; not so much riches in this world, but relationship with God; not so much our plans, but His presence—and He withholds no good thing from us because the greatest things aren't ever *things.*

He doesn't withhold Jesus from you. Christ is all your good, and He is all yours, and this is always all your miracle.

No matter the barrenness you feel, you can always have as much of Jesus as you want.

Unwrapping More of His Love in the World

Quietly, without drawing attention or fanfare, do something kind and gracious for someone in your home today.

God's gifts put man's best dreams to shame.

ELIZABETH BARRETT BROWNING

A Moment for Reflection

During what seasons of your life has God seemed most silent? Looking back, can you hear the quiet echoes of Him speaking, even during those times?

How have you sensed God's presence—His glory sparks—around you lately?

Spend time basking in God's presence, asking Him to fill your barren places with more of Himself.

Prepare the way for the Lord's coming!

MATTHEW 3:3

DECEMBER 21

The Preparations Are Already Done

Today's Reading

In those days John the Baptist came to the Judean wilderness and began preaching. His message was, "Repent of your sins and turn to God, for the Kingdom of Heaven is near." The prophet Isaiah was speaking about John when he said,

"He is a voice shouting in the wilderness,
'Prepare the way for the LORD's coming!
    Clear the road for him!'"

MATTHEW 3:1-3

The Advent road cusps.

The glow of Christmas breaches over the horizon. Everywhere, the lights signal. The music, the music drifting in—harbingers of the King.

And if you listen, linger and listen, you can hear the forerunner, John the Baptist: *The King is coming, the Lord is coming.*

The King's herald is calling His coming, calling for the clearing of the road.

You have felt that road—how it can twist, right there in your gut. Expectations can ride like highwaymen, ransacking joy, killing relationships.

Performance bandits can choke mercilessly at the jugular, steal the riches of His grace.

The herald of the King calls to you in this moment to come away from the crush and the crowds, to come away to a space of stillness to be ready for the coming of the Lord.

In the wilderness there are few roads, so Christ is the only Way.

Rest here.

The wilderness offers you grace: we are most prepared for Christ, for Christmas, when we confess we are mostly not prepared. *Rest here.* There is only room in us when we are done with us.

There is no shame in trembling a bit at the drawing near of His coming. When you have a visitation from a holy God who breathes out stars beyond our galaxy and is white-flame purity, holy awe is apt. Walk barefoot a bit through your last days of Advent. We are sinners before a holy God. But the holy God who comes is your saving God, your rescuing God, your weight-carrying God, the Shekinah glory who always splits the blackness and unleashes captives free. "God cleanses and sanctifies us, comes to us with grace and love," writes Dietrich Bonhoeffer. "God makes us happy, as only children can be happy."[27]

Rest here and happy. Rest happy as only children can be happy in the days before Christmas. Rest happy and love this story of a coming King who prepares the downtrodden for Christmas by becoming the Way, who lays Himself down in the crèche, on the Cross, so we can lie down and rest. You are unconditionally accepted and unbelievably wanted because you don't merely know of Him; you are related to Him by blood.

He comes for you in the wildernesses.

You are most prepared for Christmas when you are done trying to make your performance into the gift and instead revel in His presence as the Gift.

That is all there is left in these last days of the Advent road—the sacredness of His presence saturating everything.

You can feel it, even now.

Your Christmas becoming more.

Becoming miracle.

Unwrapping More of His Love in the World

As you make your ordinary preparations today—shopping, cleaning, baking, traveling—breathe a silent prayer, asking God to clear the way, turning your secular tasks into something sacred.

When will he come
and how will he come
and will there be warnings
and will there be thunders
and rumbling of armies
coming before him
and banners and trumpets
When will he come
and how will he come
and will we be ready

MADELEINE L'ENGLE

A Moment for Reflection

How do the performance bandits seem to target you, especially at this time of year?

......

......

......

......

......

When is the last time you rested like a child? Take a few moments of true rest today.

......

......

......

......

......

Look around you and name the sacred things among the ordinary.

......

......

......

......

......

Greetings, favored woman! The Lord is with you!

LUKE 1:28

DECEMBER 22

Be a Dwelling Space for God

Today's Reading

In the sixth month of Elizabeth's pregnancy, God sent the angel Gabriel to Nazareth, a village in Galilee, to a virgin named Mary. She was engaged to be married to a man named Joseph, a descendant of King David. Gabriel appeared to her and said, "Greetings, favored woman! The Lord is with you!"

Confused and disturbed, Mary tried to think what the angel could mean. "Don't be afraid, Mary," the angel told her, "for you have found favor with God! You will conceive and give birth to a son, and you will name him Jesus. He will be very great and will be called the Son of the Most High. The Lord God will give him the throne of his ancestor David. And he will reign over Israel forever; his Kingdom will never end!"

Mary asked the angel, "But how can this happen? I am a virgin."

The angel replied, "The Holy Spirit will come upon you, and the power of the Most High will overshadow you. So the baby to be born will be holy, and he will be called the Son of God. What's more, your relative Elizabeth has become pregnant in her old age! People used to say she was barren, but she has conceived a son and is now in her sixth month. For the word of God will never fail."

Mary responded, "I am the Lord's servant. May everything you have said about me come true." And then the angel left her.

LUKE 1:26-38

She became a space.

Mary—she opens her hands and she nods.

And the promises come true in the space of her surrender—the pod of the Most High God lodging within her willing yes.

Beneath her heart—in one yielded space—beats the thrumming love of God.

There is no need to produce or perform or perfect— simply become a place for God. That is all.

Now, here, in this juncture of time and space, God chooses the inconceivable—grace.

And conceives Himself to deliver grace into the world.

Conceive: it's not passive, but an active verb. Its root in Latin means nothing less than "to seize, to take hold of." When grace conceives in you, you take hold of God.

When you are a space to receive whatever the will of God is in this moment *as grace*, you take hold of God. You most take hold of God when you simply receive Him in this moment taking hold of you.

Taking hold of your unsure hand.

Taking hold of your unseen needs.

Taking hold of your unknown stress.

He wants to take hold of you, to be with you. He wants to carry you, to be carried by you, to have relationship with you.

The *being with* is always the gift, not merely the *doing for*. Because God knows: relationship is the only reality; there is nothing else. The way He lives in Trinity, the way we are tethered to Him, to His Body. The way He is with us and in us; the way we make space for Christ to grow us, unfold Love in us; the way the life of Christ stirs amazing grace within.

The way anywhere you make space for someone, you become a womb for God.

He comes to you as the exhausted man over a plate of cold food, the brushed-off kid in the hall, the loud woman peppering your patience with a thousand questions. When you slow and let your eyes fully receive theirs or your words nourish small things—anytime you're a safe place for another soul or you open and conceive grace—*you become a womb for God*. Nothing is impossible with Him.

Christmas is conceived in your world when you simply receive it—however Christ and His will come to you. When we think we're the ones who will have to produce Christmas, we only half-wrap the notion that we think the saving of the world begins with us. There is a name for this, and it is called idolatry.

"*No one* can *receive anything* unless *God gives it* from

heaven," says the one who is preparing the way (John 3:27, emphasis added).

Hear it like an echo of the heavenlies: Christmas can't be made, like people can't be self-made, like dreams can't be force-made. Everything is given from heaven. *Everything is a gift.* Your life becomes a masterpiece the moment you see it as a gift of grace to willingly receive.

It *is* more blessed to give than to receive—and it may be more of a struggle to receive than to give. Christmas humbles: we are not the givers we long to be. Nor are we the receivers God woos us to be.

Mary kneels before us this first Christmas not as a woman producing, performing, or perfecting but simply bending before a God who has all the power to dispatch angels, enfold Himself in embryonic cells, choreograph the paths of stars—a God who quietly beckons every man, every woman to simply come, bend, make a space, receive.

This is the chronology of grace, the chronology of Christmas: before we're called to give, we're called to receive.

This can be the hardest. We struggle to receive. Sometimes we are better givers than getters. *Grace? For me?*

I don't have to bring anything? I don't have to make anything, produce anything, perform anything? What if someone sees . . . how empty I am? How I am not enough, how my gifts

*are not enough, how giving all I've got is never enough? How
there are empty places in me, gaping places in me—all these
hollow, starving places?*

And Mary nods to you in the last days of Advent. Only
one thing is necessary—be a space for Love to come. You
simply have to receive Love. Let yourself be loved.

*Will you let Me fill all your emptiness with Love? Receive
my Love? Conceive My grace?*

It's for you.

"Nothing is more repugnant to capable, reasonable
people than grace," writes John Wesley.[28] And nothing
is harder for capable people at Christmas than to simply
come and receive.

Don't let this be the gift you refuse. *The grace is for you.*

Your greatest gift is not your gifts, but your surrendered
yes to be a space for God.

The miscarriage of Christmas begins when anxieties
crowd out space within simply to carry Christ. Make room;
be a womb. Be a womb to receive Christ everywhere, and it
is *He* who delivers everyone.

So you let the last of the trimmings go.

Cease the pace to do, buy, produce more.

Find the calendar and erase.

Somewhere make space.

And you can feel the space become a sanctuary. Sanctity stilling the crush. Glory overshadowing everything else. And time holds its breath, and the whirl of this old whirligig world holds for half a blink . . . and God comes in the fullness of His love into the willing space.

And time exhales relief, and the angels dance joy, and the velvet hush of grace received falls over this place like a coverlet over a waiting child.

Unwrapping More of His Love in the World

Take ten today. Ten minutes. Make five minutes of space and stillness and silence just with God. Then make five minutes of space in your day for someone else, and let that person fill all your attention. Invite God and His love to indwell you today.

He was created of a mother whom He created. He was carried by hands that He formed. He cried in the manger in wordless infancy. He, the Word, without whom all human eloquence is mute.

SAINT AUGUSTINE

A Moment for Reflection

Who is one person you need to make space for today—someone who has been crowded out by the busyness of the season?

What do you need to surrender to make space for Christ, to be a womb for Him?

Spend some time with God, asking Him to fill you with His all-consuming grace.

She will give birth to a son,
and they will call him Immanuel,
which means "God is with us."
MATTHEW 1:23

DECEMBER 23

God with Us

Today's Reading

This is how Jesus the Messiah was born. His mother, Mary, was engaged to be married to Joseph. But before the marriage took place, while she was still a virgin, she became pregnant through the power of the Holy Spirit. Joseph, her fiancé, was a good man and did not want to disgrace her publicly, so he decided to break the engagement quietly.

As he considered this, an angel of the Lord appeared to him in a dream. "Joseph, son of David," the angel said, "do not be afraid to take Mary as your wife. For the child within her was conceived by the Holy Spirit. And she will have a son, and you are to name him Jesus, for he will save his people from their sins."

All of this occurred to fulfill the Lord's message through his prophet:

"Look! The virgin will conceive a child!
    She will give birth to a son,
and they will call him Immanuel,
    which means 'God is with us.'"

MATTHEW 1:18-23

There are words that ring like a hammer, that split apart the atoms of things, that startle us out of the dead of sleep.

He. Will. Save.

God. With. Us.

Words with weight.

Words with the weight of glory in them, the whole of the cosmic questions—words that answer all things of gravity, that bring down the love of heaven.

This is after Mary tells him.

This is after the white heat of the Annunciation—earth and heaven and holy fire weld in a womb.

This is after the Creator, who cups the ocean depths in the hollow of His hand, folds Himself into amniotic fluid and grows bones that ache like yours.

This is after the eternal Divine without end divides in cells like bread multiplied, turns the water of the Word into blood.

This is after that.

When a carpenter dreams about the birth of God.

Mary has her angelic visitation to hear of the Incarnation weeks ago. Joseph gets only the stinging betrayal of her swelling abdomen. He gets one painfully awkward conversation. He gets to lie awake at night wondering what a nice guy like him is doing in a mess like this. No unassuming angel shows up for him until he's already made up his mind and heart to mercifully let her go. There is always that—we are not spared of all trials, but we are always spared of the trials that have no gifts.

God always gives God. Hush away the hurry, the worry. We can always have as much of God as we want.

That's what Joseph's angel says—that what is stretching Mary's skin is God. (What is always stretching us is God.)

That only the Ancient of Days has the authority to name this coming child, because the instant He inhales His first breath, He is older than His parents, older than the earth. He is Jesus; He is "the Lord Saves"; He is God with us, Immanuel.

It is Christmas that first makes the absolute claims of Christ. Like the diagnosis of a doctor, every other religion says that good-enough living will save us. But like a soul specialist, Christianity examines our hearts and says that actually we're all terminal unless we take Christ—that it's Jesus who saves us.

Every Christmas tree is shadowed by the Cross Tree: it's at the Tree that God does heart transplants—He takes your heart and does surgery.

Christianity doesn't make narrow-minded claims. It

makes a different kind of diagnosis. It's not about being narrow minded—it's about offering a different kind of medicine. In the care of our own souls, Christianity isn't so much about exclusiveness but effectiveness. *What will actually save us?*

Everyone, everywhere looks forward to Christmas. And it's the joy of Christmas that offers the gift of exclusiveness—because of its effectiveness to save the terminal soul.

He. Will. Save.

God. With. Us.

God can't stay away. This is the love story that has been coming for you since the beginning. The God who walked with us in the Garden in the cool of the evening before the Fall shattered our closeness with Him is the God who came after His people in the pillar of cloud, of fire, because He couldn't bear to let His people wander alone. He is the God who came to grieving Job as a whirlwind, a tornado, a hurricane, who covenanted to Abraham as a smoking furnace, who wildly pitched His tent with the Holy of Holies so somehow, in all His holy Shekinah glory, He could get close enough again to live amid His people. He is the God who is so for us that He can't stay away from us. The God who loves us and likes us and isn't merely 50 percent or 72.3 percent for us, but the God who is always, unequivocally, 100 percent for us—the God who so likes us, the God who is so for us that He is the God who chooses to be *with* us.

He disarms Himself of heaven so that you can take Him in arms on earth.

He comes as a Baby because He's done with the barriers.

He comes vulnerable because He knows the only way to intimacy with you is through vulnerability with you. You can't get to intimacy except through the door of vulnerability. So God throws open the door of this world—and enters as a baby. As the most vulnerable imaginable. *Because He wants unimaginable intimacy with you.*

What religion ever had a god that wanted such intimacy *with* us that He came with such vulnerability *to* us?

What God ever came so tender we could touch Him? So fragile that we could break Him? So vulnerable that His bare, beating heart could be hurt? Only the One who loves you to death.

Only the God who had to come back to get you. Only the God who would risk vulnerability, pay the price for your iniquity, because He wanted nothing less than intimacy.

It cost Him everything to be with you. Who will spend a fraction of time just to be with Him? Who wants the gift of His presence?

Christmas is about God's doing whatever it takes to be with us—and our doing whatever it takes to be with Him. He climbed down from the throne in heaven to get to you. *Climb over the throes of Christmas to get to Him.*

There are candles to be lit. There is space to be made. The stars are moving nearer now.

John Wesley died with the words "The best of all is, God is with us" on his tongue.[29]

They could beat in our hearts.

They could be the ever beat of our drum, like the ringing of a hammer, like the thrum of love coming close.

Unwrapping More of His Love in the World

Find two twigs today and construct a cross out of the bits of wood tied together with a piece of red string. Set your cross in a windowsill for you and all the world to see. Give thanks to God with us, who rebuilds us.

He, whom no infinitudes can hold, is contained within infant's age, and infant's form. Can it be, that the great "I am that I am" shrinks into our flesh? . . . What self-denial, what self-abasement, what self-emptying is here!

HENRY LAW

A Moment for Reflection

How does your perspective change on the hurry and the
worry when you remember that God is with you?

What does it mean to you that God came in the form of an
infant, with human skin?

What around you is broken and in need of saving? Ask God
to restore and redeem any broken relationships and the
broken places in your heart.

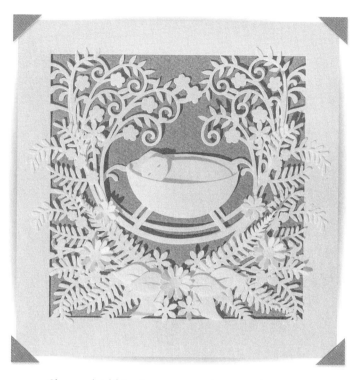

She . . . laid him in a manger, because there was
no lodging available for them.

LUKE 2:7

God in the Manger

Today's Reading

At that time the Roman emperor, Augustus, decreed that a census should be taken throughout the Roman Empire. (This was the first census taken when Quirinius was governor of Syria.) All returned to their own ancestral towns to register for this census. And because Joseph was a descendant of King David, he had to go to Bethlehem in Judea, David's ancient home. He traveled there from the village of Nazareth in Galilee. He took with him Mary, his fiancée, who was now obviously pregnant.

And while they were there, the time came for her baby to be born. She gave birth to her first child, a son. She wrapped him snugly in strips of cloth and laid him in a manger, because there was no lodging available for them.

LUKE 2:1-7

The time came. . . .

The time came quiet. . . .

All the glory had been left in heaven.

And the face of God turns one last time in the waters of the womb, and the membrane breaks and the amniotic fluid leaks and the skin of God slips naked and small and holy into hands He made.

This birth of God—who can find words? This defies words. This birth of God—this incites war.

This night, under the cover of darkness, behind the velvet curtain of silent stars—the agonies of redemption bear down loud.

This night, in the deep of the heights, as the book of Revelation tells it—and we have a revelation of all hell breaking loose and racing God to get under our skin, of an all-out cosmic war spinning across space, of the King of the forces of good driving a daring raid right into the flank of the beast who is a crimson gash tearing the waiting sky.

The Nativity of this night is a brutality of heaven and earth.

In the heavenlies, according to the Nativity of Revelation, the child breeches, the beast lunges, and our eyes flash away, too terrified to witness evil devouring holiness and our one last hope.

All of earth holds its desperate, wild breath.

And then, at the last possible moment of all this impossible, the Infant is seized and thrust to the throne. The Child lives! Rescue is certain! And all of hell makes one last lunge, clashes desperate, the dark horde of evil wrestling Michael and the heavenly host—and then it's over. Satan falls like lightning from heaven, falls out of the sky in a heap.

And now over Bethlehem, in the Nativity according to Luke, the star hangs high, victorious on a silent night, a holy night.

Now all is calm.

God comes. . . .

God comes quiet. . . .

This night a battle has been waged and won for you. Love had to come back for you. Love had to get to you. The Love that has been coming for you since the beginning—He slays dragons for you. This is the truest love story of history, and it's His-Story, and it's for you. All the other fairy-tale love stories only echo your yearning for this truest, realest one—this one that has its beginning before the beginning of time. This night, you on this visited planet, your rescue is here. You can breathe.

Your God extends now on straw.

He lays Himself down in your mire.

He unfolds Himself in the stench you want to hide, in that mess that is your impossible, in the mucked straw you don't want anyone to know.

Rejected at the inn, holy God comes in small to where you feel rejected and small. God is with you now. Wherever you are—in a soundless cry or hidden brokenness or in your ache—God always wants to be with you. You are not ever left alone in this. We are never left alone in this; God is with us.

This is Love you can't comprehend. You can only feel and touch this kind. There, in the place where you feel rejected, you can be touched by God. There, in the places you feel small, you can touch God. He came in the flesh.

Come kneel close.

Let the warm breath of heaven fall on you.

God waits to be held.

God waits for you to draw close.

Grace is weightless.

God comes as a Babe because grace is weightless.

On a chilled night under stars, there is no grand mass of people whose efforts pry the stars into place. In an obscure caved barn, down some backstreet of Bethlehem, there is no great host whose good works unlatch heaven and impress God into coming. Tonight, at the foot of the cradle of Christ, like at the foot of the Cross of Christ, there are no big people—no powerful, no proud. Tonight there are only those who tramp to the manger with nothing; there are only the manger tramps, the men who lay down all the self-made, the women who lay down all the self-sufficiency, the children who lay down all the wants. We, the manger tramps, who kneel where thrones tremble and demons fall and the self-made crumble and the self-righteous weep.

Tonight there are only the manger tramps, who tramp in with all our poverty of spirit . . . so there can be an abundance of God.

And the bulk of all your worn shreds slip off the weariness of your back.

You have tried to polish enough for Him with these rags. You have tried to patch together so much for Him. You have tried to produce too much for Him with these rags.

And you—we—who are the manger tramps see it tonight, what He's written in red on all our filthy rags: *But I did it for love.*

All of conquered heaven and grateful earth echo and throb tonight with the heart cry of the God-Child: *I did it for love.*

What can all the manger tramps do but wrap the vulnerable God in strips of our bare, broken hearts so He can lodge in the intimacy of us?

The greatest Gift laid into our empty hands. . . .

Grace is weightless.

Even the winning stars singing it over the manger tramps tonight.

Unwrapping More of His Love in the World

Put on your shoes and go for a walk today. Sing a Christmas carol out loud. Go into all of the world and tell one person about the greatest Gift and how He loves.

Christmas is fast approaching. And now that Christ has aroused our seasonal expectations, he'll soon fulfill them all!

SAINT AUGUSTINE

A Moment for Reflection

What do you need to lay down so your hands will be open to receive God's Gift?

How does it change Christmas for you to know that Jesus did it for love?

Take a moment to kneel close at the manger, thanking God for His abundance.

The Savior—yes, the Messiah, the Lord—
has been born today!

LUKE 2:11

DECEMBER 25

Today

Today's Reading

"The Savior—yes, the Messiah, the Lord—has been born today in Bethlehem, the city of David! And you will recognize him by this sign: You will find a baby wrapped snugly in strips of cloth, lying in a manger."

Suddenly, the angel was joined by a vast host of others—the armies of heaven—praising God and saying,

"Glory to God in highest heaven,
and peace on earth to those with whom God
is pleased." . . .

[The shepherds] hurried to the village and found Mary and Joseph. And there was the baby, lying in the manger. After seeing him, the shepherds told everyone what had happened and what the angel had said to them about this child. All who heard the shepherds' story were astonished, but Mary kept all these things in her heart and thought about them often.

LUKE 2:11-19

The heavens dome different this day, the light all different.

The glory's rising—glory to God in the highest heaven, and peace on earth, because God has left the glory of the galaxies and come down to our depths.

God is here! God is here! Christ is born to *you*, to *you*! The glad tidings are to *you*, to *you*!

It's like you can hear the beating of angel wings over Bethlehem—a whole vast host—as if the sky lifts with a light that isn't of the sun or of the stars or of this world.

Angels leaned in near the mystery so large that has become the Babe so small, and they caught Light, like catching fire.

One star hovered too close to the infinite God-become-infant and combusted bright.

And the flame of it all grazed the shepherds up on the hills, and they blazed, full of wonder, to the source—to the stable where the star seemed dim in the incarnated brilliance of the Light of the World.

God, divine Light, tabernacles Himself in skin and lights the darkness of men.

Jesus left the starry heavens to save us from our sins.

This day, this night—this is the time of the awed silence.

Now, a thousand thousand trees dance with light.

Now, a thousand thousand gifts carry love.

Now, at the foot of every tree, we are all only recipients of grace.

Christ, who called all things into being, gives you sun and moon and stars, the earth under you and the sky over you, and this ocean of air for every breath that fills every lung of every living thing—to you, to you, to you! *We live in an ocean of grace. Gifts are our air.*

And when we sinned and weren't satisfied with what God gives, as if we refused to breathe air and died, when we longed for something different, something more, something better, He came and *gave us Himself.*

Am I enough?

Jesu, joy of man's desiring.

Love birthed Himself and births us life.

I'll take your broken heart and give you My warmed one; I'll take your broken body and give you My fresh Spirit; I'll take your burden-broken back and give you weightlessness.

Take Me? Let Me be your enough? Always now, no matter what—let Me be your enough.

You can have this as the best Christmas ever as much as you gaze into your Father's face and receive His gift.

"Only He who has experienced it can believe what the love of Jesus Christ is," whispers the pen of Bernard of Clairvaux.

A heart could burn with a love like this.

The whole of the journey, the whole of the Scriptures, is of Him. "Did not our hearts burn within us?" (Luke 24:32, ESV).

This day, this night, the Light comes, and whose heart isn't kindled by this Love that's a wildfire? The shepherds got angels, were lit by the angels. Everyone else that night got shepherds, heard the news from kindled, heart-burning shepherds who went and "told everyone." When your heart burns, you're a flaming match for other hearts. When you're a manger tramp who came with nothing but your ragged heart and leaned in close over that crèche, when you've beheld His glory, the white heat of a Love like this— who doesn't tramp out of the manger and into the world with a heart glowing like hot embers in your chest?

A heart like this could catch the world on fire.

Christ came into the world for you—and you came into the world for Him.

The world will be still tonight.

There will be lingering. Longing. We will long for this wonder to all go on. One Christmas candle will flame in the quiet. This cannot fade—none of this can ever fade. "For unto us a Child is born, unto us a Son is given" (Isaiah 9:6, NKJV). *God is with us.*

God stays with us.

The Christmas candle burns hot, gives its light, gives its Light—and the world lights up, and Christmas goes on forever now.

Christ, the always Gift for all our days.

Notes

1. John Calvin, quoted in William J. Bouwsma, *John Calvin: A Sixteenth-Century Portrait* (New York: Oxford University Press, 1988), 103.
2. Ann Voskamp, *One Thousand Gifts: A Dare to Live Fully Right Where You Are* (Grand Rapids, MI: Zondervan, 2010), 15.
3. Charles Spurgeon, "God's First Words to the First Sinner" (sermon, Metropolitan Tabernacle, Newington, England, October 6, 1861), http://www.ccel.org/ccel/spurgeon/sermons07.lvii.html.
4. Nicholas Wolterstorff, *Lament for a Son* (Grand Rapids, MI: Wm. B. Eerdmans Publishing Co., 1987), 90.
5. Charles Spurgeon, "Abraham's Double Blessing" (sermon, Metropolitan Tabernacle, Newington, England, November 8, 1885), http://www.ccel.org/ccel/spurgeon/sermons43.xxvi.html.
6. Dwight L. Moody, *The Way to God* (New York: Cosimo, Inc., 2005), 53.
7. G. K. Chesterton, *Orthodoxy* (New York: Simon & Brown, 2012), 163.
8. Voskamp, *One Thousand Gifts*, 161.
9. Chesterton, *Orthodoxy*, 121.
10. Elisabeth Elliot, *Love Has a Price Tag: Inspiring Stories That Will Open Your Heart to Life's Little Miracles* (Ventura, CA: Regal Books, 2005), 206.
11. Thomas Watson, *A Divine Cordial; the Saint's Spiritual Delight; the Holy Eucharist; and Other Treatises* (The Religious Tract Society, 1846), 68.
12. *The Christian Armor with Illustrative Selections in Prose and Poetry* (Boston: The American Tract Society, 1865), 133.
13. John Owen, *Hebrews*. The Crossway Classic Commentaires, edited by Alister McGrath and J. I. Packer (Wheaton, IL: Crossway Books, 1998), 234.
14. Voskamp, *One Thousand Gifts*, 203.
15. Jonathan Edwards, *The Works of Jonathan Edwards*, vol. 1 (New York: Daniel Appleton and Co., 1835), 664.
16. Amy Carmichael, *Edges of His Ways: Daily Devotional Notes* (Fort Washington, PA: CLC Publications, 2011), 82.
17. C. S. Lewis, *The Great Divorce* (New York: HarperCollins, 2001), 83.
18. G. K. Chesterton, *Tremendous Trifles* (New York: Dodd, Mead and Company, 1920), vi.

19. Carl Sagan, *Pale Blue Dot: A Vision of the Human Future in Space* (New York: Ballantine Books, 1997), 7.

20. Ibid.

21. Dr. Timothy J. Keller, "Fire on the Mountain" (sermon, Redeemer Presbyterian Church, New York City, September 19, 1999), http://sermons.redeemer.com/store/index.cfm?fuseaction=product.display&product_ID=17335&ParentCat=6.

22. C. S. Lewis, *Mere Christianity* (New York: HarperCollins, 1980), 28.

23. J. R. R. Tolkien, *On Fairy-Stories*, edited by Verlyn Flieger and Douglas A. Anderson (New York: HarperCollins, 2008), 75, 78.

24. J. R. R. Tolkien, *The Return of the King* (New York: Del Rey, 2012), 246.

25. Arthur T. Pierson, *George Müller of Bristol* (Peabody, MA: Hendrickson Publishers, 2008), 404.

26. Charles Spurgeon, "A People Prepared for the Lord" (sermon, Metropolitan Tabernacle, Newington, England, March 13, 1887), http://www.spurgeon.org/sermons/2404.htm.

27. Dietrich Bonhoeffer, *A Testament to Freedom: The Essential Writings of Dietrich Bonhoeffer,* edited by Geffrey B. Kelly and F. Burton Nelson (New York: HarperCollins, 1995), 185–86.

28. John Wesley, quoted in David L. Larsen, *The Evangelism Mandate: Recovering the Centrality of Gospel Preaching* (Grand Rapids, MI: Kregel Publications, 1992), 155.

29. "History: John Wesley, Charles Wesley," *Westminster Abbey,* http://www.westminster-abbey.org/our-history/people/john-wesley,-charles-wesley.

THE ART OF THE GIFT

As you and your family celebrate the coming of Christ this Advent season, I invite you to download the exquisitely designed ornaments featured in this book from my website to adorn your own Jesse Tree. I pray they will be a perennial reminder of the true miracle of Christmas and of God's greatest Gift to us.

—*Ann Voskamp*

www.aholyexperience.com

(Use code JESSE)